Faith

Does It Really Move Mountains?

Judy Baus

AmErica House
Baltimore

First printing

ISBN: 1-58851-072-7
PUBLISHED BY
AMERICA HOUSE BOOK PUBLISHERS
www.publishamerica.com
Baltimore

Printed in the United States of America

A special thanks to:

Mom who has stood by me through thick and thin! She always has just the right FAITH words to speak at the exact time I need them.

My husband who has persevered through our journey of FAITH. Speaking only words of FAITH during the rough times.

My Editor, Lynda Johnson who has spent hours with me to perfect and produce a book on FAITH, that is balanced and practical.

Marie Holt who is the administrator for Good News Ministries, Inc., and has been faithful in helping me stand in FAITH for many years.

My son who has become one of the great FAITH teachers!

Finally to all who have prayed and encouraged me to not quit, but keep on pressing on living the life of FAITH.

CONTENTS

Editor's Note

Editing Judy's book on faith has been both a challenge and a blessing. Each time I would start working on the book, I'd look at it as an editor and correct, rearrange and whittle away. But before long, questions like "Where are you with God?" and "What are you trusting the Lord for?" pierced my mind and spirit, causing me to put the pencil down and do business with God.

One of the overriding themes through the book is about doubt and unbelief—major problems for many believers. Judy gives example after example of how she stood firm on what God said in His Word and saw Him change herself, her family and situation after situation.

In her first book, *From Rags to Riches*, Judy tells her story of how God brought her from the life of a hopeless alcoholic to that of a committed and joyful believer in Christ. In this book, she tells the keys of how that can happen for *anyone* who is willing to be honest with God and open and teachable. Her example is an inspiration for us to more diligently get in the Word, stand on specific Scriptures for our situations and watch it work for us, too.

Each time I worked on the book, I could feel my faith-level rising. My prayer is that this will be the same for each reader today... that you will take time with the book and allow the Spirit to bring healing to any areas of need in your life. You'll read in this book that much of the faith-life is our responsibility. Not God's. And also, stepping out of our comfort zone. Who wants that? But once we do it, we'll find how much more exciting our life will become because as Judy says, being a Christian should be fun.

Whatever you are going through, I trust as you read this book, you will grasp onto the supernatural God-faith and see it move mountains in your life.

Lynda Johnson
Writer/Editor
Communications and Marketing
Partners International

Introduction

The Bible is the Christian's manual for success and, simply put, if we live God's way, we will win; if we do not live God's way, we will lose. We want to be winners in life, so let's take a fresh look at God's principles for being winners. It all starts and ends with faith, the working kind of faith that pleases God, and penetrates our life with truth.

Hebrews 11:6 says, *Without faith it is impossible to please Him,* and in Romans 14:23, *...for whatever is not from faith is sin.* Hebrews 10:38 says, *Now the just shall live by faith; but if anyone draws back, My soul has no pleasure in him.* Jesus asked in Luke 18:8, *...when the Son of Man comes, will He really find faith on the earth?* Just from these Scriptures alone we see that faith is a very important subject. We must walk by faith and not by sight, so if everything we do must be in faith, how do we get faith? What is faith? What makes it work?

We can find many different books on the subject of faith. The most informative and usable faith books that I have found are those where the authors have used the Bible as their main source of reference, backing it with application. Most of them (me included) have the same foundational Scripture references to teach us how to apply faith in our lives. Why? Because these Scriptures are the best examples we have from the Word of God to present truth on the subject of faith.

2 Timothy 3:16,17 says, *All Scripture is given by inspiration of God, and is profitable for doctrine, for reproof, for correction, for instruction in righteousness, that the man of God may be complete, thoroughly equipped for every good work.* My main goal for writing this book is to see that men and women of God have a workable, active understanding of faith. My desire is not just to repeat the very familiar faith Scriptures to you because, as King Solomon wrote hundreds of years ago, *there is nothing new under the sun* (Ecclesiastes 1:9). We all agree with King Solomon, but I hope to expand and bring some fresh insight to what God is saying to us about faith through His Word.

I realize that there will be people reading this book who are right in the middle of a crisis, or who will be going through one. If we aren't in a crisis now, I know that on this side of heaven we will all go through crisis situations at one time or another, and we all have our levels of faith. This book is not intended in any way to bring condemnation on anyone, but to simply give insight to the inexhaustible subject of faith. I tell people everywhere I go that God wants us to be honest about where we are in the things of God. After Adam had been disobedient to what God told him to do in the Garden of Eden, he hid from God. God asked Adam in Genesis 3:9 "Where are you?" God knew where he was and he knows where we are, but He still asks the same question to each of us today, "Where are you?" We, like Adam, must locate where we are with the things of God. When we look at God's Word with open, teachable, and honest hearts, God will show us the adjustments we need to make in our walk with Him.

Faith is a foundational truth of Christianity. We can't even believe in God without Him giving us faith to do so. We are all given the same measure of faith, so why are some people more victorious than others? Have they found some "Christian secret" that I can't seem to find? I hope to answer these questions on the following pages. We will look in depth at Scriptures on faith and at the lives of men and women of faith, both from the past and the present. What has God called you to do? If you don't know now, you will. One thing is for sure; we must have a living, active faith to be victorious in our Christian walk.

I do not have all the answers to the many questions on the inexhaustible subject of faith, but neither does anyone else. So read with me, chew on the meat and spit out the bones. If you are open, teachable, and honest, I know that you will move higher in your faith level.

Chapter 1
WHAT IS FAITH?
Faith stands; hope reels it in

Our foundational Scripture is Hebrews 11:1: *Now faith is the substance of things hoped for, the evidence of things not seen.* I memorized this when I first became a Christian, but I didn't understand it until much later. The word "faith" is in the present tense meaning *now.* Faith (Greek word *Pistis*) is a word that means confidence or a firm conviction. The word "substance" means foundation, confidence, or assurance. What are the "things" mentioned in this Scripture? Well, what do you need? I did not say want! What concerns you? The word "hope" in this verse is future. It means to anticipate with pleasure. The word "evidence" means proof. Now here is the big one. It says of things NOT seen. My faith right now will bring things from the realm of the not seeing to the realm of seeing at a future time. "Faith is NOW– Hope is FUTURE." If I can see it, if I can do it, and if I can take care of it myself, I do not need faith for it. This is not faith. So many people miss this key right here because if they don't see something happening right away, they quit. So faith is not some "pie in the sky" theory that God dangles at us, seeing if we can grab onto it. He does all He can for us to have faith, but we have our part to do also.

We must decide intellectually to believe in something or someone. It is an act of our will. We need facts to rest upon. God provides the facts, but we must exercise our free will and believe. We need faith or belief for everything important in our lives—salvation of our families, healing of our marriage, health, money to pay for the things we need, God's direction—for everything.

Faith pleases God. Hebrews 11:6 tells us, *...without faith it is impossible to please Him, for he who comes to God must believe that He is, and that He is a rewarder of those who diligently seek Him.* Faith is a gift. In the United States, we are raised on a merit system so it is hard for our minds to comprehend something of value given to us freely. Jesus came and died on a cross for us freely. Freely we may receive that gift of life, eternal life as we receive Jesus and believe in Him. When we have done that, then we receive freely this gift of faith.

We must believe or have confidence that God is who He says He is, and that He will do what

He says He will do. The only way we are going to know this is to know His will. In order to know His will, we must know His Word. God's will is His Word. It all goes together! To diligently seek God is to search out, investigate, or to crave after Him. This is what pleases or is acceptable to God.

Believe (Greek word *Pisteuo*) is the verb form of faith and means to be fully persuaded or trust in. When we are in this position it says that God will reward us. "You mean to tell me, Judy, that we get rewards?" What does the Scripture say? Yes, God rewards our diligence as we seek Him by faith and come to a place of trust and being fully persuaded that God is who He says He is, no matter what problem or situation I am in. This is what pleases or is acceptable to God.

In Acts 16:31 they (Paul and Silas) spoke, *...believe (or have faith) in the Lord Jesus Christ, and you will be saved, you and your household.* When I was first saved, my marriage was a mess and after I was saved, it was still a mess. I knew that God did not want me to divorce (I had been there and done that before I came to Christ). The Bible is either true or it is not true, and I chose to believe God for "my household." I also found the Scriptures, which showed me that the children of

Israel were told to get ready to leave Egypt; God was going to release them from their bondage. They were to take a "lamb for the household," kill it and eat it, but they were also to take the blood of the lamb and put it on the two doorposts and on the lintel of the house where they ate the lamb. This is an overview of Exodus 12:7. The slaying of the lamb represents the slaying of the Lamb of God on Calvary's cross for our household. With these Scriptures fully placed in my mind, I told the devil he would not have my marriage or my family, and when I said that, the fight was on. I had the precious promises of God to stand on. I had my covenant rights, and I exercised them against the devil. I waited six years in faith believing that my husband would come into the kingdom of God. No one or no thing could have convinced me differently. It took work, but guess who was helping me–the Lord!

God wants us to exercise our faith in practical ways. Every Sunday and Wednesday evening for one year, I saved a seat next to me for my husband. I went to the pastor and got permission to do that. The deacons and ushers helped me stand in faith for my husband and would not allow anyone to take that seat next to me. It did not matter how full the church was, no one sat there. Some of my brothers and sisters in the Lord were not happy with that. One even said, "I need that seat; your husband is never going to come to God." Boy, did I need to release that comment to God. I did not receive that statement because it was scripturally not correct. God wants no one to die without knowing Him, and I knew that included my husband. So I just continued to save that seat with my Bible beside me. Then one Wednesday night in walked my husband right through the church doors and down that aisle to sit next to me. Boy, did people start to save seats for their loved ones. The only problem was that they got tired and took the Bible off the saved seat too soon. We stop standing in faith right on the brink of a miracle. Don't quit just because of how something looks, feels, or what someone may say. Believe God for your miracle. I did, and in God's perfect time, He brought forth that miracle in my husband's life.

My husband loves to fish and as I watch the process of this wonderful sport, I have observed that our faith is like his fishing pole. He is NOW hanging on to that pole firmly, and he casts the line in the water. His pole is like our faith. The object of fishing is catching and he knows that fish are in the water but he can't see them. How does he know that there are fish in that water? Because, others are catching fish around him. It is just a matter of time and he shall catch one. He must wait and not quit, but that is his choice. All of a sudden his pole bends and he has his fish. He uses the reel on his pole to bring it in. His reel on his pole is like our hope. With every turn of the reel he anticipates with expectation that the fish is going to be a whopper. He has gone from fishing to catching, but it took time to get the fish out of water to the shore–faith will stand; hope will reel it in! Some fish are harder to get on shore than others, but eventually they all will be brought to shore.

Faith is always producing a confession of God's promises that will produce a surrender of our will to His. This will cause us to take action and become doers instead of just hearers! With all this in place our hope will bring it in.

Chapter 2
BENEFITS OF FAITH
**God loads us up daily with benefits and
at the same time He tells us
not to forget them**

Psalm 103:2 says, *...forget NOT all His benefits* and 68:19 says, *...who DAILY loads us with benefits, the God of our salvation! Selah* (which means to pause-stop and think about this.) This excites me but saddens me at the same time. God loads us up daily with benefits and at the same time He tells us not to forget them. That shows me that I can forget my benefits. Faith is a benefit of our salvation. Sad but true, I have been guilty of forgetting about this wonderful benefit of faith, and because of my forgetting I have brought trouble upon myself every time.

Through faith we receive many things because of our salvation from the Lord. Ephesians 2:8 tells us, *For by grace you have been saved through faith....* The Greek word for "saved" is *sozo* which means, "to heal, cure, preserve, keep safe and sound, rescue from danger or destruction and deliver."

My husband, Vic, and I have had many opportunities to be rescued from danger, especially when we are on the road. We travel full time in the ministry in a greyhound bus we converted into a motor home. One time we were going down the freeway and a truck carrying four-by-four boards dropped one on the road. A truck in front of us hit the board, shooting it end first in our direction. Right before this happened I had an overwhelming urgency to pray. I did just that, and about three minutes into the prayer, this board hit right above my side of the front window. The reader board for the destination of our bus reads HEAVEN, and that board hit right beside that sign, causing a big dent. Had it hit three feet lower, it would have gone right through me. Yes, one aspect of our salvation is "rescue from danger."

So we are saved by faith and we *live by faith.* Hebrews 10:38 records, *Now the just shall live by faith, but if anyone draws back My soul has no pleasure in him.* It says the "just," meaning a born-again believer, "shall," meaning now, "live," meaning everything we do must be done by faith. We also go a step further. "But if anyone draws back" …from what? From faith! If we draw back from living by faith, God says, "My soul has no pleasure in him." Those are strong words. Drawing back is like stepping backwards instead of stepping forward. The children of Israel came out of Egypt by the signs and wonders of God, but when they were supposed to go into the promise land, they drew back from the faith that would have caused them to go into this land flowing with milk and honey. The decision to draw back killed everyone over 20 years of age.

Enoch is an example of going forward and he went forward so much and pleased God so much that he just walked right into heaven. He had faith to be translated, it says in the Hebrews hall of heroes (Hebrews 11). The book of Hebrews is not about the hall of fame, but the hall of faith. They were heroes because they had faith. We must always be careful what comes out of our mouth. Words like "It will always be like this, nothing will ever change," or negative words about our situation that go against the Word of God are not faith words. God is not pleased with that. He wants us to always believe that He is the God of the impossible. If it is in the will of our Father, nothing is impossible. We always have a choice to draw back or go forward and believe God. When I first started to write books, I would get right to the publishing of the book and then I would want to draw back from faith. The benefit of faith tells me God is able to help me finish what we had started. The choice of faith was mine alone.

Every step that we take is to be by faith. 2 Corinthians 5:7 says, *For we walk by faith and not by sight.* We are not to look at the things going on around us with our natural eyes; rather we are to see them through the eyes of faith. The first time Vic and I set out on our adventure with God, I really had to apply this principle of seeing the trip through the eyes of faith. I had never traveled much nor did I desire to. Now I go with my husband to unknown places and people. As I go, I say, "Okay God, you have to help me do this." Through the eyes of faith, I say I need to see people turning to Him, encouraged in Him. He is faithful, and on the way back home, I feel like a runner crossing the finish line. I'm jumping in the spirit. Each trip I trust Him more and more and can see through the eyes of faith clearer each time.

God's Word will open our hearts to receive. Romans 10:17 says, *Faith comes by hearing and hearing by the Word of God.* The word "hearing" is present tense, meaning over and over again. It's a continual thing. It doesn't say faith comes by "having heard" or "going to hear." It says, by hearing, right now. That's why it's important to hear the Word of God being spoken and to study the Word of God ourselves. I make it a practice to read the Word of God out loud, because then I am speaking it and hearing it, and my faith level will increase... or decrease if I am hearing and speaking things against what God says.

I believe Romans 10:9 is the most foundational lesson on the importance and power of confessing faith. *That if you confess with your mouth the Lord Jesus and believe in your heart that God has raised Him from the dead, you will be saved.* The Holy Spirit establishes this principle at the very beginning of our lives in Christ. We have eternal life because of confessing with our mouth and believing with our heart. So His continual working in our lives is advanced by the same means—by confessing the name of Jesus and His promises. It is also by believing in our heart that God's Word is true and that He is all He says He is.

So we have a principle for all of our life beginning in the Spirit of saving faith. The moment we are saved we have an active working covenant with our heavenly Father. Let us grow to active faith. How do we do this? By believing in God's mighty power for all of our needs, speaking with our lips what our hearts receive, and believing the promises that are in His Word. Let us accept God's covenant for all of our needs by empowering it with what we are allowing to come out of our mouth. We need to keep hearing the Word, putting it in our spirit, and have it come out our mouth. Choose carefully your closer friends. Who you hang around with is who you will be like! Don't be silly and think your faith level will stay high by hanging around with doubt and unbelief. It can't and it won't. Faith will produce faith. Doubt will produce doubt. Let us not forget the benefits of faith that we are daily loaded with.

Chapter 3
GOD IS NOT PARTIAL
Since faith can grow, we can have more or less, great or small

Everyone is given the same measure of faith when we are saved. *For I say through the grace given to me, to everyone who is among you, not to think of himself more highly than he ought to think, but to think soberly, as God has dealt to each one a measure of faith* (Romans 12:3). Everyone is "dealt," which means appropriated or distributed to each of us the same measure of faith. When does this measure of faith come to us? It comes to us when we become part of the kingdom of God, which comes when we are born-again according to the words of Jesus in John 3:3-5. God is not a God who is partial. He gives us all the same measure of the supernatural God-kind of faith. The word "measure" means a limited portion or a certain size by a fixed standard. Every child of God starts with the same amount of faith.

We will find the same word for faith when we read about the fruit of faith in Galatians 5:22, and the gift of faith in 1 Corinthians 12:9. The gift of faith found in 1 Corinthians is simply that—a gift given to us by the Holy Spirit when we need it. Gifts are given, but fruit is grown. The faith that is dealt to us in the beginning of our Christian walk is a fruit of faith that must be developed. As we yield to the Holy Spirit and learn to exercise our faith, it will grow. Orchard growers tell us that the fruit does not appear on the tree fully grown. It is developed over a period of time. A gift of faith can be prayed for, but everyday faith that we need for everyday living is a fruit of the Holy Spirit and that has to be grown. If we are children of God, we have faith. We need to use our faith and watch it grow and mature.

I remember when I was a manicurist, I was given a little plaque that said something like "Put your trust in God." I was not very bold at that time, but I put that little plaque on my table and a woman walking by saw it and stopped. She started to cry, and said she needed to know more about God! I told her about God and she became a believer. Boy, did my faith level grow by just stepping out with my faith and putting that plaque up.

Since faith can grow, we can have more or less, great or small. *We are bound to thank God always for you brethren, as it is fitting, because your faith grows exceedingly*... (2 Thessalonians 1:3). Our faith can grow exceedingly. I like that. I looked up the word "exceedingly" in Webster's dictionary and it means a high or exceptional degree. Strong's dictionary says, to increase to above ordinary. My faith can become exceptional, but I have to use the measure God has given to me. Faith is like a muscle. If you do not use a muscle, it will shrivel up to nothing, but if you exercise a muscle, it will get hard and firm. My dad had a long-term illness and passed on because of the illness. This was before I was saved so I knew nothing of faith or prayer, but I did know that muscles needed to be used or they would be lost. It was because of the constant massage of my dad's muscles that he was able to get out of bed during this illness. He had excellent skin and wonderful muscle tone even at the point of his death. Why? Because of keeping the muscles active in his body by massage. This is the same with our faith. Our faith needs constant use if we are to keep it steadfast and firm. We do this by standing on the Word of God and trusting the Word to work in our lives.

John G. Lake was a great man of faith in the early 1900's. He was a very successful businessman who cut ties with the business world to launch out on a faith journey with God. He, together with his wife, seven children, and a missionary team headed off to Africa. Rev. Lake and his wife wanted to trust God for their care so they had disposed of their money before leaving. It is told that they had $1.25 in their pockets, and did not have a clue where they would stay on arrival in Africa. By the time they all stepped off the ship in Cape Town, South Africa, about two weeks later, Rev. Lake had been given money plus a fully-furnished house in Johannesburg. He was a stranger in the land, but he watched God do a bundle of miracles. Within eighteen months of his arrival, it is said that he had started his church in Johannesburg plus over 100 other churches in the surrounding areas.

He did something with the measure of faith given to him. It grew to become exceptional and certainly above the ordinary, and he became known as the Apostle of Faith in South Africa. I am not advocating that we should all go and dispose of our money, but could it be that Rev. Lake had relied on his money too much? I believe this is why he gave it away. He wanted to use his faith and watch it produce for not only him but also those around him.

There was a time when, like Rev. Lake, I had

to learn to believe God for a certain amount of money to run this ministry. Now that the ministry has grown, we have to believe God for more money to meet the expenses. It has been a process of growing in our faith. Remember, when God gives you a vision, He will also give you the provision to complete the vision. People ask me, "Judy, where do I start?" Start where you are.

Chapter 4
START SMALL AND WORK UP
Start making faith a habit

Everybody starts with the same measure of faith. We must all start with small faith and work our way up to great faith. How did the great men and women of faith do it? They had a key. A key will unlock and open something, and the key they used was the Word of God.

John G. Lake was a student of the Word. He was born in Ontario, Canada, and was one of sixteen children. He grew up with a strange digestive disease that almost killed him. He lost eight of his siblings. His memories were filled with the cries of his parents as he experienced funerals, tears, and grief. His over exposure to sickness and sorrow sparked in him a rare and intense desire for God. This drove him to find a way to beat sickness, disease, and even death itself. He had to experience the power of God. The struggle he had was choosing between getting down to business with God, or getting down to business with the world. One turning point in his life was choosing to get down to business with God. After many years in Africa he came back to America. He landed in Spokane, Washington, where he rented a suite of rooms. They were called the "Divine Healing Institute." This institute became known around the world as the famous "Healing Rooms." Rev. Lake was known for having his Bible either in his hand or within close range. It is said that he always kept a pencil and paper handy to write the things down that he was learning. People say that he studied the Bible so much at night that it got to where his wife had to learn to sleep with the light on.

Smith Wigglesworth was an English preacher who always had a Bible in his pocket. He did not feel properly dressed if he did not have his Bible. It is said that wherever he was after a meal, he would pull out his Bible and read from it to feed his spirit.

Maria Woodworth-Etter ministered with signs and wonders following her preaching. She was born in New Lisbon, Ohio, and founded a church in West Indianapolis, Indiana. She was married and had six children. She experienced the pain of having five of them die at a very early age. The tragedies in her life pushed her forward into a close walk with Jesus. She traveled to places and set up meetings where people told her, "no one is going to come." The Holy Spirit would come and bring people from all around. Believing the Word of God, she stepped out in faith to do what God wanted her to do in a time when it was not popular to be a woman in the ministry.

These are just a few great men and women of faith in the early 1900's, but we can read throughout church history of many others who all started the same way. It didn't matter if they were rich or poor, male or female, they all had to start with their faith the same way. They started small and worked up to great faith. Each of them told of their love for the Word of God. They learned that, in order for them to do great exploits for God, they had to know the Word of God. Just as these great men and women of faith learned to feed their spirits, so must we.

If we do not eat the proper food, our bodies will suffer. Some people live only on junk food and their bodies show it. Well, what about our spirit man? Junk food is a huge problem to our spirit man. If we want our faith to grow into exceptional and above-ordinary faith, we will have to feed it often. We will also have to feed it healthy faith food. We must get off the junk food! When we are in our Bibles, praying, and listening to the Word of God being taught, we are feeding our spirit man. We will then experience our faith growing bigger and bigger.

While we were in Wyoming doing some ministry work, I was watching a family of robins. I watched the babies grow stronger and stronger until finally they flew away by themselves. That did not happen overnight. They had to learn to feed themselves and fly. I watched how the mother robin did all the feeding while they were in the nest and even for a period of time when they were out of the nest. But the time came when she had to turn them loose to do what they had been taught. There were two birds from the same nest, but they were so different. One did not want to dig worms for its food. It did not want to fly, but only wanted to be taken care of. This bird would just sit screeching for help. At one point my husband even gave it one of his fishing worms. Finally, after many hours of screeching, the baby knew that if it did not do something, it would starve to death or get eaten by another animal. Finally it decided to try, and found out that it could find good food and become strong enough to fly. Where was the mother bird during this process? She was sitting on a nearby branch and watching all the time.

She knew that if her baby were to survive in this world, it would have to quit screeching and help itself. This is so like our faith and our heavenly Father. He gave us all the same measure of faith and He is watching to see what we are going to do with it. We have to try to use our faith, but we must have the proper faith food to get strong enough to trust God's Word; then our faith will grow and work for us.

If God had demanded that we have faith when it was impossible for us to have faith, we would have a right to challenge His justice, but He places in our hands the means whereby faith can be produced. The responsibility is ours whether or not we have faith. I can't blame God if I don't have faith; it is my fault! Faith must be fed and developed. It takes time and everybody is at a different place in their belief level.

We have to start at the beginning in our faith walk. If we need a new car, and we are believing for a Mercedes, but our bank account only covers a Volkswagen and our faith is there for a Volkswagen, start with a Volkswagen. Later, if God sees that we need a Mercedes, then we can stretch our faith for that. When this ministry first started, Vic and I needed a motor home to fulfill the vision. We started to believe God for a bus.

We got that bus, a 1953 Greyhound, and we converted it into a beautiful motor home. Now it is time for a newer bus so we are once again believing God for this. This time we are believing for a bigger and better bus, but we are ready for that. We need it to reach the people we believe God wants us to reach for Jesus here in the United States.

Faith is like a seed. It must be planted, watered, watched over, cared for. It is something that produces much bigger than at its conception. Take a mustard seed. Planted and handled carefully, it will grow into a tremendous plant. An acorn, handled right, will grow into a mighty oak tree. My mom has a prune orchard and in order for the trees to produce good fruit, they have to be taken care of properly. I remember when the orchard was first planted and the trees were small. They were so small that Mom could prune each one of them by herself each year. These trees did not produce fruit for several years, but they still had to have a lot of care. Mom had to water, prune, and fertilize these trees even though they were too young to produce fruit. She knew if she continued to nurture the trees that someday they would produce an abundance of fruit.

Start making faith a habit. We must first make a *decision* to use the faith given to us. This is a choice that no one can make for us. We have to first decide. Then we need to be *determined* that no matter what happens, we shall believe God. Next comes the hardest of all and that is discipline. It takes *discipline*. We need to discipline our lives in every area. We have to make the time to read the Word, and make the time for prayer. God must be first in our lives. I learned a long time ago to get up early and make Him first in my life. I wouldn't think of leaving the house before I talked to my heavenly Father, read His Word, and saw what He wanted me to do that day. Lastly, we must be *diligent* which is being consistent with our faith. As we experience life and put faith principles to work, we will overcome and we will grow.

God is good. He always wants to help us if we will only ask Him. The more time we spend in fellowship with God the Father, Son, and the Holy Spirit, the more we will see our circumstances and people from the Father's perspective and through the eyes of faith.

Chapter 5
FAITH TAKES WORK!
Jesus has already won the victory for us,
but we have to enforce that victory

Don't misunderstand the title of this chapter. We are saved by grace, and the only way we receive salvation is to believe in Jesus Christ as our Savior. We are not saved by work! But after salvation, we have something to do. Our faith doesn't come easy! We must *fight the good fight of faith, lay hold on eternal life, to which you were also called and have confessed the good confession in the presence of many witnesses* (I Timothy 6:12). A "good" fight means we win, but in this case, not by natural means. The fight must be in the spirit realm and it is by faith. We have to learn how to do that. Jesus has already won the victory for us but we have to enforce that victory. The good fight of faith is just that—by faith. The good fight of faith will not be won in the physical realm of what we see, hear, smell, touch, and feel or, in other words, with our physical bodies. The good fight of faith will not be won in the soul realm with our intellect. It is a spiritual battle and can only be won in the spirit realm.

For the weapons of our warfare are not carnal but mighty in God for pulling down strongholds, casting down arguments and every high thing that exalts itself against the knowledge of God, bringing every thought into captivity to the obedience of Christ (2 Corinthians 10:4,5).

We are a spirit, we have a soul (mind, will, emotion), and we live in a body. We will not win unless we fight the good fight of faith God's way! Remember, the devil wants your faith. Carnal weapons are worldly weapons! They are physical and intellectual. Satan knows you will lose every time when you bring the fight out of the spirit realm. Have faith in the spiritual realm and then it will manifest in the natural realm. Many people have it backwards and that is against the principles of faith. You must play by God's rules! We live by faith and not by sight!

When Vic and I became believers in Christ, we each had our own businesses in Reno–he was a carpenter and I was a manicurist. Eventually we felt the Lord's leading us to sell our businesses, leave Nevada and go to Bible College. So we did. We went to California with no jobs lined up, just a strong knowledge that we were in God's will. We had to trust God and step out on our faith.

God was faithful with everything, but there was a huge battle to win. I knew that God was on our side and that we would win if we stood our ground with the devil.

Vic spent weeks trying to find a job; he sent out more than 100 resumes. We kept having to remember how God had led us thus far, and the reality that we were not fighting a battle with flesh and blood. We battled in the spirit realm with the Word of God as our sword. Eventually Vic found just the right job, one with flexible hours where he could attend classes and still have some time to study.

James 5:15 says, ...*the prayer of faith will save the sick, and the Lord will raise him up....* When we pray in faith we quench the attacks of the enemy. It may not happen instantly, but it will happen. We are to pray and it is the Lord's job to raise up. God is in charge of the way the healing will come, and the time the healing will come. The Lord may first need to make some adjustments in the person's life. I have been healed many times. Each time the Holy Spirit has shown me where I needed to adjust something in my life. I have had to make spiritual adjustment, physical adjustment, and intellectual adjustment. The problem has always been with me; it will never be with God. Sometimes we forget that and blame God for what is not His fault at all. The Bible is true and we serve a God who does not lie. We have a God of compassion and love. Do not allow the enemy to discourage you; just keep on praying!

Ephesians 6:16 says, *Above all, taking the shield of faith with which you will be able to quench all the fiery darts of the wicked one.* When this was written many of the shields were made out of some type of leather, which had to be conditioned and treated regularly with oil to keep them from getting dry and cracking. Then when the fiery darts came from their enemies, they would not stick but slide off. If the shield was allowed to become dry it would be set on fire by the enemies' attacks. The shield was to protect soldiers but they had to work at keeping their shields in proper working order. It is the same with the shield of faith. It must be cared for on a regular basis. Yes, the enemy's fiery darts will come, but God has made a way for us to pour water on them and that is with the shield of faith. This is the only way that pleases God. So how important is faith? Without faith we are of no use to anyone, and we surely will not be winners.

Before my son was saved, he had a drug

problem. But I believed God. I took that shield of faith and every time the enemy told me, "Why are you praying? He will always be the way he is because you didn't teach him about God," I would put up that shield of faith and not look at what I saw in the natural. I would hang on to the promise of God that I *and my household* would serve the Lord.

Another definition of faith is, "A consistent, conscious decision that develops into a conditioned response." It is a habit we must form. We must consciously decide to respond in faith every time a situation comes our way. We condition our minds and discipline ourselves so that we respond rather than react. How do we respond? We respond with acts of faith.

Before I came to know the Lord, I was an alcoholic. Notice I said WAS! It is a lie to say once an alcoholic, always an alcoholic. Satan wants to bind us, but God wants to set us free. Can we believe God for freedom from addictions? I did and God delivered me. I have not had a drink for over fifteen years. We can stand on the Word of God for our needs. I replaced the habit of drinking with the habit of praying and reading the Word. I put feet to my faith. Did it take work and discipline? IT

CERTAINLY DID!

Hebrews 11:1 in the Amplified reads, *Now faith is the assurance (the confirmation, the title deed) of the things (we) hoped for, being the proof of things (we) do not see and the conviction of their reality (faith perceiving as real fact what is not revealed to the senses).* What is proof? In a court of law, proof is evidence, a testimony. "Hope" is an expectation or a confidence. I can trust in it. The root word for hope in the Greek means to anticipate with pleasure. Hope is future. We can't see it, but it is out there. If we can see something, we don't need to have faith for it. It is already there. We must see it in our mind's eye, in the spirit realm. If we are having trouble with sickness, we must see ourselves off the sickbed and well. If we are in financial debt, we must see ourselves prosperous. Even though we are right in the middle of that circumstance, we have to see ourselves out of that condition. See it exactly as the Word tells us.

People say to me, "Judy, I am not going to lie about my situation." Who said lie? I said speak what the Bible says, and that is truth. Many times I have said, "I am healed and the devil is trying to make me sick." That is truth! I am holding that shield of faith up, and praying the prayer of faith. The Lord will raise me up!

When I receive a bad report, I say, "No way! What does God say about that report?" I only want God's prognosis. Several years ago I was having problems with my gums and teeth so I went to a periodontist. I received a bad report from him so I got in the Word to see what God wanted in that situation. This bad report was not of God!

I had three choices: Have my teeth pulled, have surgery, or trust God. Since I knew this bad report was not of God, and since I obviously didn't want surgery, I chose the latter and stood on the Word. I knew that my God could heal me. I was not denying that I had gum problems, but I was confessing that Jesus Christ was my Lord and my healer. I was confessing that the word *salvation* means healing, and I was standing on the fact that God had already healed me when Jesus took the stripes on His back for me. So I was going to see my gums whole with my mind's eye.

I also asked God to show me if I had been the cause of my problem. I asked Him how I needed to adjust myself. He showed me three things: I was not getting enough rest; I was not eating properly; and I was allowing stress to come into my life, rather than letting Him take it from me.

He showed me that I not only had to trust Him, but also had to allow Him to make some very important changes in my life. I did both and my teeth tightened up and my gums were healed. I received the miracle. Several years later I had the problem surface again, and I had to seek the Lord's wisdom once again.

I was not *denying* the devil's work, but *defying* the devil's work. There is a BIG difference. It was faith calling out for hope, and commanding it to come to me. This kind of faith calls things that are not, as if they are. They have already happened. Look again at Hebrews 11:1. It says faith is *now*, not going to be, not yesterday was, not tomorrow will be, but it says NOW faith is the assurance. The assurance, the title deed; the confirmation of the things we hope for. We can't see it, but it is there. As we see it in our spirit, we call it forth.

When we go out to fight the good fight of faith, we need to know that we cannot be lazy! It doesn't matter what we need from God, we are going to have to take a stand and fight for it. The devil does not want us to be a winner. It takes work to be a fighter.

The Roman soldiers would go out with their full armor on and so should we if we want to win. We must put God's armor on and keep it on to win. Ephesians 6:11-17 says the WHOLE armor, not just part of it. The devil has armor also. We will have one or the other. We will either be girded up with TRUTH or with lies, have the breastplate of RIGHTEOUSNESS or wickedness, feet shod with the preparation of the gospel of PEACE or preparation of the gospel of enmity, strife, and discord, shield of FAITH or the shield of doubt, the helmet of SALVATION or the helmet of damnation, and the SWORD of the Spirit which is the WORD OF GOD or the sword of evil imaginations. The WHOLE armor of God takes work to keep it in place and secured, but to have the shield of faith in place and not the rest of God's armor will leave us open to lose. We can't win the fight of faith by putting on any part of the devil's armor! We are saved by faith and the grace of God, but after that we have a part. Faith takes work!

Chapter 6
STEPPING OUT OF OUR COMFORT ZONE
**God did not tell us it would be easy,
but He did tell us
He would be with us through it all**

The Bible records many examples of people who stepped out in faith. Abraham is called the Father of our Faith. He is a strong example of a person who exercised his faith, *and it was credited unto him for righteousness* (see Romans 4:1-3). Abraham didn't just agree, but he trusted God and relied on Him (and he didn't have even one copy of the Bible on his shelf!). Believing will cause action. Believing will put feet to what we want or need, and action will produce results.

Abraham and Sarah were to leave everything that they had and step out into an unknown territory, unfamiliar ground. Vic and I also did this when we left our home and places of business to change states and go to Bible school. Then following graduation from Bible school, we left to travel the highways and byways reaching people for Christ. This was all unknown territory to us. Genesis 12:4 says, *So Abram departed as the Lord had spoken to him....*

Abraham (formerly called Abram) was not young. He was seventy-five years old when he departed from his land. That's faith! When Vic and I left Reno, I was in my mid-40s and I thought that was old. We are never too old to trust and believe God to bring us to the destiny He has for us, but we have to step out of our comfort zone. People said to us all the time, "How can you do that? You have a comfortable life, and don't forget you are not getting any younger. What about your retirement?" We were given all the "what ifs" and "woes". Change is not comfortable. Change is not easy because we are a people who like ease and comfort. God did not tell us it would be easy, but He did tell us He would be with us through it all.

Even if the situation is bad, some people still prefer to stay where they are rather than to go forward to the unknown. That is why so many people stay in abusive situations because they are familiar with where they are. The unknown of tomorrow is too hard for them. This is sad to say, but true! As children of God we must get rid of that comfort-zone mentality and go when and where God wants us to go. We must always seek wise counsel, but God has the final say!

When we read the account of Abraham and Sarah we can see they made a lot of mistakes, but they obeyed God's voice. They trusted Him. We are in the mission field and we must trust God even with our mistakes as we do the best we know to obey Him. Have I made mistakes? Oh my, yes! But I never allowed that to stop me. If my motives have been correct and my heart is after God, I know that my heavenly Father will handle my mistakes. God has the ability, but He needs our availability.

The Lord said of Abraham, …*I have made you a father of many nations…* (Romans 4:17). That was a prophetic word from God. Prophecy is conditional. The word is circling in heaven. Doubt and unbelief, sin and skepticism will not allow the Word to mature. Believe the Word and be obedient. Live it, believe it.

Words create pictures. I had a prophetic word from God that I would be in ministry full time traveling the United States and preaching the Word of God. At that time I was a manicurist and had no plan to quit, travel, or preach. That was in 1988 and by 1990 everything was in motion. But I had to believe and be obedient to the Word when I saw it unfolding.

Romans 4:17 says, ...*call those things which do not exist as though they did.* That's what Abraham and Sarah did. They believed God. The Greek word for believe is *pisteuo* which means "to trust, rely on, to be confident or fully persuaded" that everything that God says is truly going to happen.

When I knew that I was called into ministry, I was fully convinced of it. I waited for it to happen. I did not try to make it happen, but I was obedient to every step that God wanted us to do. Because of that we watched God open doors. So the prophetic word was in heaven circling around waiting for me to fulfill all the conditions of the prophecy. I knew that God wanted us to start a storehouse for the needy, a place where we could gather clothing and food for those in need. This ministry started with a plate of food given to a homeless person. God placed the prophetic word in our hearts, and we had to fulfill the conditions of it. We had to build the storehouse before it could be filled. The word would not have been fulfilled had we not submitted to the conditions of it. Usually it means work! Salvation is a free gift, but after that, work is involved to fulfill the purposes of God.

Now verse 18 says, ...*who, contrary to hope, in hope believed*.... So contrary to hope– ordinary human expectation, Abraham expected God would fulfill His promise. Natural senses told him that he was past productivity. Experts would have told him there was no hope. You're too old to have children. Sarah is too old to have children, and in their day every woman wanted a child. Children brought honor to the family name. God gave Abraham the promise, but God knew that it would take Abraham's wife, Sarah, in agreement with her husband to bring the promise to pass. Sarah had to have faith and hope also. If Abraham was going to be a father of many nations, who was going to be the mother? Sarah! They had to feel they were swimming upstream while they were standing in faith and hoping for this promised child to come forth. It is always easier to go with the flow of doubt and reasoning of why something can't happen than to believe God that it will come to pass. Sarah even laughed when she heard what God had said. She heard with her natural ear that told her NO WAY!

Sarah's greatest dream was to have a child after all those years of being barren. Her natural thinking was saying, "I am old and my husband is old." She had grown comfortable in not having a child, and had long ago given up on her dream to have a child to carry on the family name. Now God was asking her to step out of that comfort zone with Abraham. The Lord had given them a promise of a child, so now against that natural hope of what anyone would have said, Abraham and Sarah hoped in God. That's Godly hope. Supernatural hope! God's hope says, I'm going to stand in faith (faith is now, hope is future), and I am going to believe the Word of God, not all the reports that come in. I'm going to stand, believe, and obey everything that God says. I know that it's going to come to pass.

There is no hope in the dark. Hope turns on a light and you can see it. Why? Because biblical HOPE means *to anticipate with pleasure.* You will have to see what you need with faith to anticipate it with pleasure. There is no such thing as blind faith. Hope gives us a vision and it lays hold of faith. Paul says don't beat the air. Hope reels it in, and faith grabs hold of it. Hope is specific, not generic. It has a target. It has a clear picture. You hope first, then believe. Grab hold of that.

What are you hoping for? What do you need? What are you waiting for? We had a need in this ministry for a computer. I was standing in faith for it. I didn't tell everyone about the need, but God knew we needed this. Whatever you need to fulfill God's call, He will give it to you as you stand in faith believing. He will provide. We hoped for that computer, believed for it, and stood in faith for it. We got it! With Abraham there was no productivity in his organs or in Sarah's. God worked a creative miracle. Not by the faith of God, but by the obedience of Abraham and Sarah. If they had not been obedient, it would not have come to pass. God has so much to give us, but He wants us to exercise our faith to appropriate His promises.

Romans 4:20 says that Abraham *did not waiver (or stagger) at the promise of God through unbelief....* Faith cannot work with double-mindedness. A drunk person will stagger or waiver, unsure of his footing. Unbelief is like that, like cheap booze, making you unsure of your footing. The police have a test that they give a person who they think has been drinking and driving. The test is to walk a straight line. This is very simple to do if we are not drunk. I know because before Christ came into my life, I had been there and done that. Likewise, unbelief will cause us not to walk the straight line of faith. Verse 20 continues, ...*but (he) was strengthened in faith, giving glory to God.* Faith will bring us strength. As we stand in faith, we'll get stronger and stronger. Faith always gives glory to God.

Verse 21 says Abraham was *fully convinced that what He had promised He was also able to perform.* Here it is in a nutshell. I was fully convinced that my husband and my son were going to come into the kingdom of God. I could not be persuaded any other way no matter what happened or what was said. I knew that it was God's will to save them, and I had His promise that He would. If God promises it, He is able to perform it! That's where we need to get. We need to be fully convinced. We just say Amen, so be it, and there's no argument. We don't have to believe the doctor's diagnosis or the doctor's prognosis. I don't care what the hospital says or what anybody says. The diagnosis and the prognosis are God's alone. Christ is our healer and provider. The Bible is full of promises for us, and we can stand on that. You and I need to remember how Abraham and Sarah handled "impossible" situations.

It is safe to sit in a church pew, and we ALL need to sit in that pew for a time. But God designed each of us to also step out to do what He has called us to do. We all have a call and that is to share the gospel with those who do not know Him. We all have a commission. Within that commission we all have a vision or destiny that God has given to us. It is by faith that we are going to bring that vision in. Are we going to go through things? Yes. Are we going to make mistakes? Yes. Are we going to fail? Of course we are, but failure is not quitting. Failure is just an opportunity to see God work in our life. We pick ourselves up and brush ourselves off and go on.

The Apostle Peter failed Jesus and denied Him three times. Peter got beyond his failure and went on after the Resurrection and Ascension of Jesus to help start the church and bring thousands into the kingdom of God. He had failed but did not allow it to keep him down. Now the Apostle Judas was a different story. He also failed Jesus by turning Him over to His enemies, but Judas could not get beyond his failure. He quit! I see no difference in their failures, but there was a difference in the way they handled failure. Failure is just an opportunity to see Jesus help us through it and beyond it.

God is a good God, and He is for our highest success. I believe Judas could have gone on to be a great leader in the early church had he not given up because of a mistake he made. He allowed his remorse of that failure to push him to suicide. Jesus would have helped Judas with his faith to overcome failure the same as He had done for Peter, but Jesus was not given the opportunity.

Living in this age is a training ground for each of us. This is boot camp. We are soldiers in training. We are learning how to become effective soldiers in combat. Every child of God is in combat but every child of God is not effective in that combat. We have won the war, but we can see many people losing the battle! I understand that the battle is the Lord's, which means we will win if we do it His way. We might be going to heaven, but we have a lot to do here before we get there. He is building His army and He is the Commander and Chief, leading us in and through if we listen to His instruction. We need our faith strong to do that.

Genuine faith is that which is still standing after the artificial layers have been stripped away by trials and testing. We need to know that God wants us to succeed at what He has called us to do, and to succeed we must step out of our comfort zone by faith.

So when we are stepping out doing what He has called us to do, believing for things that belong to us, Jesus our High Priest is praying for us that our faith won't fail. We can never base our faith on someone else's experience, but we always base our faith on Jesus Christ and His Word. He has already won the victory for us, and all we have to do is enforce the victory that He has provided.

Chapter 7
THE LANGUAGE OF FAITH
Like any language, it has to be learned

Faith is a language we need to learn. When we go to a foreign country we have to learn the language of the land if we want to communicate with the people. Even here in the United States, words mean different things in different regions. I have to learn how to communicate with people in different regions. Some words in one area might mean something slightly different in another area. Also, my language is English, but I can't use English to speak to someone who only speaks Spanish. I would need an interpreter in order to be effective or learn their language before I speak.

We go to a doctor and he speaks a language we don't really understand. We look at the prescription he writes, and we wonder what it means. Only the pharmacist knows because he understands the language. Computer talk is also a special language. When I first sat down to a computer, I didn't have a clue how it worked. I had to learn the language of that computer. I had been using a word processor before I received my first computer. I had them side by side many times. One night I was learning to work my computer and had entered twelve pages of notes for a class I was completing. I lost all of it. The paper was due very soon. I had a choice to go back and redo the paper on the word processor, which I knew how to use very well, or to proceed with this new computer. I knew that my heavenly Father wanted me to learn how to use this new wonderful computer, but He still gave me the choice. New or old? Take your pick. One is the easy way, the familiar way, and the other way takes patience and persistence, but will be to my advantage in the long run. I picked the new computer, and I can tell you it was to my advantage.

My husband is a carpenter and has special tools he uses to build fine cabinets. If he doesn't have the right tools or speak the language of carpenters, he won't succeed. As a manicurist, I used fingernail files on my clients, but my husband couldn't use that kind of file for his cabinet. He had to use a wood file! It is the same with faith. We have to speak faith words, not doubt and unbelief, but sureties. We have sureties because we have the Word of God. It may seem like denial, but it is not. It is standing firmly on the promises of the Word of God.

If you are having trouble with marriage, sickness, poverty, relationships, or addiction–all of these things are changeable. There are times when I look at my checkbook and I see nothing in it, but as soon as I go to the bank and deposit some money, that will change the balance in my checkbook. It is true that I have no money in the bank but that truth can be changed. That is worldly truth. But eternal truth is not changeable. The Lord says let the weak say I am strong. God says He will cause my hands to prosper in all that I put them to do. Look at the Word of God and find a promise or a truth and stand on it. When a worldly report comes, know that it is changeable. The Holy Spirit brings hope to us and we see it through the eyes of faith. We must see with our spirit what we are hoping for before we will get it. The language of faith only speaks eternal truth. When we are children of God we can speak this faith language. Like any language, it has to be learned; this takes time, hard work, and lots of practice. It is the same with the faith language. We have a choice to make in every situation, whether to speak the language of faith or the language of the world, doubt and disbelief.

Look in the mirror each morning and tell yourself, "I am more than a conqueror through Christ," "I am the head and not the tail!" and "I can do all things through Christ who strengthens me." If God has called you to do something, YOU CAN DO IT. Positive affirmations? Yes, but they are more than that. They are what God says about us. They are the language of faith.

Chapter 8
THE POWER OF WORDS
AND WORDS OF POWER
We have heaven or hell
in the power of our mouth

By His own word the Lord spoke creation into being (see Genesis 1) and *by His word he sends healing, saving and deliverance* (Psalm 107:20). These and many other Scriptures speak of the power of God's Word. God's Word is power and there is power in His Word. And the Word of God took on personality in the person of Jesus. *In the beginning was the Word, and the Word was with God, and the Word was God* (John 1:1).

The words coming out of our mouths have the capability of great blessing or great cursing—evil or good is in our mouth. We know that words can cut down or build up. They can have widespread influence on everything. Proverbs 6:2 says, *You are snared by the words of your mouth.…* In other words, you are taken or defeated by the words of your mouth. Do you ever say in frustration or anger, "I'll never be able to do that," or "I can't do anything right"? Our words have an affect on ourselves and on others. Choose them carefully. Words from the wicked spread like wildfire. Good words bring good fruit. Either way, they have an affect.

Proverbs 10:11 reads, *The mouth of the righteous is a well of life, but violence covers the mouth of the wicked.* How do murders take place? Usually by violent words, arguments, a lack of self-control. How about road rage? We are hearing more and more about this. Some people get very violent behind the wheel of a car. They yell and scream because they are in a hurry and they think the person in the other car is going too slow. Their mouth has become wicked, which will lead them to violence, sometimes even to the extent of physical harm to others or themselves. Many years back the word "righteous" was spelled right-wise-ness. I feel this way of saying righteousness is better because that is what righteousness means. Right-wise-ness in our thinking, talking, acting, and motives. We should have right-wise-ness coming out of our mouth so it will be a well of life to us and others. I have many opportunities to choose to use right words when confronted with angry people. We all get angry, but it is how we handle the anger that makes the difference.

A man will be satisfied with good by the fruit of his mouth...(Proverbs 12:14). Are we not satisfied with good? Let's take a moment to reflect on what has been coming out of our mouth. What fruit are we speaking? Is the fruit coming out of our mouth love, joy, peace, patience, kindness, faithfulness, goodness, and self-control?

Matthew 12:36,37 says, But I say to you that for every idle word men may speak, they will give account of it in the day of judgment. For by your words you will be justified, and by your words you will be condemned.

What are idle words? They are nonproductive words. When we or others are in trouble, are we speaking productive words which will bring life, healing, wholeness, or are we speaking idle chit-chat? I say chit-chat because that is what it is. Our help cannot come from the world, only from the Word of God. Jesus says we will be judged by our words.

He who guards his mouth preserves his life, but he who opens wide his lips shall have destruction (Proverbs 13:3). Can't you just picture that? I love the Lord's vivid way of getting His points across.

Death and life are in the power of the tongue, and those who love it will eat its fruit (Proverbs 18:21). We have to be careful what words we communicate. We are presenting Jesus to the world and we need to paint a picture with our words. Job said, *How forceful are right words…*(Job 6:25). Job spoke fear and it came upon him (3:25). Those things that he feared, he got.

Let's quit talking about what we can or cannot do, but talk rather about how the greater One lives within us. Go against the world. Don't go with the world. Say, "I'm going to have a great year! I don't care what anybody says." No matter what happens to the economy, we look to God as our source. Our jobs are not our source. Yes, God works through our jobs, but my paycheck, when I had a paycheck, was not my source. God is my source. That is not being arrogant. It is simply believing God. I am not totally living all of that yet, but I'm holding fast to it and will continue to grow towards it. Every local fellowship or itinerate ministry like ours needs money to go forward and fulfill what God wants done through them. I have always had to be careful not to get a "mailbox mentality." A mailbox mentality is when we start to see what comes to us through the mailbox as our source! Faith people keep their eyes on God as their source, but with the understanding that He does use people to meet the needs of the ministry.

People who "talk faith" stand out. They are

not agreeing with the world. They are not agreeing with systems and circumstances. How about David? David was about sixteen years old when he confronted Goliath. Negative words filled the minds of the people in the Israelites' camp. *"The giant is big and ugly and he's going to kill us!"* All the soldiers and all of David's brothers were talking that way. David said, "Who is this guy who defies the army of the living God?" David had spent much time with the Lord and could see the situation, including Goliath, from God's perspective. He acted on that and defeated the enemy. Faith is like seed. Our inside is the bin holding a measure of faith (whether it be big or small), and our mouth is the planter.

We are living today what we created yesterday with our mouth. *Out of the abundance of the heart, the mouth speaks* (Luke 6:45). *A merry heart does good, like medicine* (Proverbs 17:22). Medicine is a treatment used to treat a disease; a merry heart is that treatment for that diseased part. I have heard that we use more muscles in our face to frown than we do to smile. Interesting, isn't it? We are full of faith, or we are full of doubt and disbelief. We have the power of life and death in our tongues. James says out of the same mouth proceeds blessing and cursing. This ought not to be. Jesus says by your words you are blessed or you are condemned. We have heaven or hell in the power of our mouth.

It is hard to know people unless they talk. As we listen to them, we will know where they are spiritually. Words are containers. When we are in a squeezed situation, what is in us comes out of our mouth. Our words affect people. They are containers of faith or fear, of life or death. We need to take a tape recorder twenty-four hours a day, and have it on all the time to see what is in our mouth. That is a scary thought.

My mom has twenty acres of prune trees, which is her source of income. Five different times we have seen the enemy put death threats on those trees, and five different times we have seen the Word of God work as we confess it, or profess it out over the orchard. As we prophetically speak the Word of God, before it happens, we watch it pierce the heavens and manifest in the natural. We have seen God heal the root system and stop the wind on our behalf. We have seen creative miracles as God has had His mighty hand on this orchard. Did He do it? Yes, He did it through the spoken word that we professed over the orchard, that it would live and not die for the glory of God.

Why can we stand on that? Because my mother is a widow; she is a child of God. The Word of God says He will take care of the widows. It says that He is our provider. He saves us from destruction and rescues us from danger. He will cause our hands to prosper. We look up all these Scriptures and we stand on them. We can confidently say to the enemy, "Go back from where you came and loose these trees, in Jesus name!" You have to stand and refuse to believe the report of the natural circumstances. Only believe the report of the Lord. So we spoke over the orchard for the glory of God. There's your key. It is for God's glory because it belongs to Him. We held fast and we couldn't be moved. Pressures will come; temptations will come to try to make us turn the other way.

One year a strong wind came through Mom's orchard and took out about 350 trees. With 350 trees less, God still provided a high yield of fruit. Then for two years in a row she had almost no crop due to the weather. She did get enough prunes to pay the expense of running the orchard all year but nothing to live on for the year. During those years we were not moved by what we saw, but we stood on the promises of God to provide for her and keep her. We stood in faith and experienced God's provision to come and it did abundantly and above what she imagined.

We have to stand in the midst of our circumstances and have joy in tribulation when the pressure comes. We have to hang on to what the Bible says, and not go by what we feel.

Chapter 9
MEDITATION GOD'S WAY
Chew on it, ponder over it, pound it in

Joshua 1:8 says, *This Book of the Law shall not depart from your mouth, but you shall meditate in it day and night, that you may observe to do according to all that is written in it. For then you will make your way prosperous, and then you will have good success.* To the world, the word meditate has a different connotation than it does to Christians. Some teach that meditation means to sit and say "Ohmmmmmmm" and empty your mind and wait for thoughts to come in. That is not what meditation means here.

This word meditation means to drive in, like pounding in. It is like a cow chewing her cud. She swallows it and then brings it up again, chews it, swallows it, and brings it up again. The Word of God is like that. We are to get every bit of the nutrients out of it. How long do we chew on the Word of God? Until we get it. We just keep chewing, and chewing, and chewing. It is like food. Jesus said, *"the food I have is to do the will of the Father"* (John 4:34). Psalm 34:8 says, *Taste and see that the Lord is good.* As we meditate on Scripture we need to think about chewing on it, pondering over it, pounding it in. Allow the Scripture to go over and over in your mind. If you need healing, take healing Scriptures and allow them to become part of you. Whatever concerns you, Scriptures can be found to help you through it. Whatever you need to complete your journey through life here on earth, the principles of recovery are the same! Only by allowing the Scriptures to become part of you will you discover recovery. The answers are found in our manual of success, "The Bible." We can't meditate on our car manual to fix our lives. The right manual must become part of us to have success in life. I can study my typewriter manual all day when I am fixing my computer, but my computer will remain broken. Wrong manual! It is the same with the things of God.

The more you think on something, the more you become like the thing you are thinking on. What are you thinking about–TV, sports, latest styles? Whatever we are thinking becomes a part of us. God knows that, so He says keep the Word of God before us night and day, meditating on it.

In his book, James says we are to find joy in our trials, and Paul says in 2 Corinthians 7:4 ...*I am exceedingly joyful in all our tribulations,* but how can we do this? We live in a fallen world and tribulation is going to come, but as these things come in on us and we exercise faith in God, we will grow. Tribulation means trouble or persecution, not sickness and disease! It is our responsibility to enforce the victory in God. We will see Him change things, and we will learn to *respond* in situations rather than *react.* God is interested in our character. We are becoming effective soldiers in the kingdom of God. We are to live by faith, not sight, in every step we take. When we wake up in the morning we should dedicate the day to God and ask God to direct our steps. Then we will step by faith with Him into the unknown.

We do not know what is going to happen in the course of the day. That is why God said, *"Therefore do not worry about tomorrow, for tomorrow will worry about its own things. Sufficient for the day is its own trouble"* (Matthew 6:34). If we get up and meditate on this Word, the Word will go from our head to our spirit. That way we can continue to allow the Holy Spirit to direct us. We don't have to know what is going to happen, we just have to know, have confidence, have trust, and believe that God is for our highest success. We have the promises of the Word of God. When we know that we have met the conditions of God, we must then step out on the promises of God. As we experience things we will grow.

The greatest growth that Vic and I have had is when we stepped out into full-time ministry. We have seen God move situations, move those mountains on our behalf and we have grown from each experience. If we had not gone through all those trials and tribulations of setting up a ministry, of not knowing where we were going day to day, we would not have been able to experience the miracle-working power of God in our lives. We meditated on the Word; then we did what the Word said to do! Writing my first book **From Rags to Riches** was not easy. I had never written a book before and I didn't even know how to start. I needed great faith, so I started to meditate on the Scriptures, which told me who I am in Christ. I started pondering and chewing on the words, *I can do all things through Christ who strengthens me* (Philippians 4:13). I knew God wanted me to write the book to allow Him to change lives through it. So I meditated on Scriptures, then I had to step out and do it. Was it easy? No! But because of meditation, I had God's Word deep in me, and my faith grew stronger and stronger each day as I applied it to my life.

Proverbs 4:20-21 says, *My son, give attention to my words; incline your ear to my sayings. Do not let them depart from your eyes; keep them in the midst of your heart; for they are life to those who find them, and health to all their flesh.* We have to keep the Word before our eyes at all times and see what we need. As we keep our spirits fed with the Word, we give attention to the Word of God. We incline our ear to the saying, but we must make sure we are really listening. We can be sitting in a service listening with our ears, but not hearing with our mind. We have to catch it with our spirits. As God's truth becomes real to us, it is going to be health to our bones and life to our flesh, which means every part of us.

debt. We used the Word of God and stood on our faith. God did not send an anonymous check in the mail, but he did help both of us build up our businesses and pay off our debts. We are now totally out of debt. I have had the Lord also heal problems in my neck, my sinuses, my back, and my hand. My gum problem was a big one and God took care of that. When we left to go to Bible school we left our jobs—the only sources of income we had known for most of our lives. And now we have the bus as our home and we travel full time in the ministry. Our faith is growing each day. As we exercise our faith, stand on those things of God and say there will be fruit, it will come forth. God has given us authority over those mountains in our lives. We have seen it come forth.

It is easier for me to believe for things now than it was in the beginning of this walk of faith. It has become a way of life. We cannot believe for the removing of cancer if we have never believed for the removing of a headache. Pretty soon we will believe for more and more, and then we will believe for things we never thought we could. What is in our hearts comes out of our mouths—it is either doubt and unbelief, or faith.

Again, it is not praying and it is not asking.

Jesus says learn how to speak to those things ourselves. Sometimes we don't know how to get things out of our life so we say, "God, you do it." We say, "Father, I need this taken care of and that taken care of." To God, this would be like my asking a very experienced author to write my book for me. God says, "No, I am not going to do it for you. I have given you all the authority to do it. I have told you how to do it. You have the Bible to show you how. You have My words to back you." God says YOU SPEAK IT and I WILL ENFORCE IT. That makes it fun. Christianity should be fun.

Jesus challenges us to stretch our faith and trust Him for more than we can imagine. *Now to Him who is able to do exceedingly abundantly above all that we ask or think, according to the power that works in us...*(Ephesians 3:20). Abundantly means exceedingly overflowing, and above ALL that we ask or think. God is the Creator, NOT Santa Claus! Sometimes as I listen to people, I know that this is forgotten. He enforces things spoken that are in His will and the Word is His will. We need to think before we speak and make sure that our words are spoken with the right motive behind them. Silly talk and greed go nowhere with God. God provides through His covenant agreement with us overflowing from us to others. What is that power that works in us? It is the Holy Spirit's power, that faith power. Jesus beckons us to raise our level of faith. Only God's Word, empowered by the Holy Spirit, can do that.

Chapter 11
ONE ENEMY TO FAITH–FEAR
We have to see God
bigger than our situation

The devil is not afraid of us, but true people of faith create a problem for him. The devil doesn't care if we go to church. We can go to church every day of the week if we want to. What he cares about is faith. When we step out in faith and do something, the devil gets concerned. Jesus tells us in John 10:10, *The thief does not come except to steal, and to kill, and to destroy. I have come that they may have life, and that they may have it more abundantly.* That word abundantly means 'excessive,' 'overflowing,' 'surplus,' 'more than enough,' 'extraordinary,' and 'more than sufficient.' The Christian life should have an overflowing of abundance. What does the enemy want to kill, steal, and destroy? Our faith. So what is faith? It is our assurance, our conviction, and our title deed. It will grow faster in some areas than others.

We all have our mountains, our obstacles to overcome, but we have to see God bigger than our situation. 1 John 4:4 says, *You are of God, little children, and have overcome them, because He who is in you is greater than he who is in the world.* Very early in my walk with the Lord I memorized this Scripture and each time I read it or say it, more depth of the meaning comes to me. We really should stop right here and meditate on " YOU ARE OF GOD." That is a powerful statement. If we would only get that fact and it is a fact, if you have asked Jesus to take over your life. 2 Peter 1:4 says, *...been given to us exceedingly great and precious promises, that through THESE you may be partakers of the divine nature.* We partake in His divine nature? Wow, that should make us shout for joy. If God is for us, who can be against us? I tell people all the time to repeat this over and over until they get it deep inside them. We are of God! Before I understood or knew many Scriptures, I had this one down inside me, and it kept me through all the turmoil that was going on in my life.

I believe God when He says I have overcome them, meaning the enemy, because greater is the Holy Spirit that is in me than the enemy that is in the world. We must get these Scriptures in our heart so that we will be able to stand on them when the enemy comes to rob us of our victory and joy. Every time my husband and I step out in faith, preaching and teaching, feeding the homeless, and encouraging the Body of Christ, we know the enemy is going to hurl his darts at us. He challenges our faith; he wants us to pull the plug on our faith. But we know that the greater One lives within us, and He will help us overcome.

Every fear is a doubt of one or more of God's promises. When we walk in fear, we are saying that God doesn't have the ability to pull us out, or that God's promises are going to fail. When I fear for the salvation of my children, I'm saying that God's promises are not true. When I fear for my health, I'm saying God's promises are not true. Finances, God's promises aren't true. However, Jesus came to deliver us from fear.

Fear is the number one thing the enemy tries to get us into. He says, "Hath God really said?" casting doubt. Then we think that we didn't hear right or we didn't see right. Remember, *Satan can't do anything to us when we are not in fear, any more than God can do something for us when we do not have faith.* This is really simple. These are opposing forces. We must ask the Holy Spirit to reveal to us fear in our life. If these are opposing forces then I certainly do not want fear opposing my faith.

Vic and I were on our way to do a weeklong conference in Winnsboro, Louisiana, when my back went into such muscle spasms, I could not move. We were one day from our destination and I could not even get out of bed to dress, let alone minister for a week. What was I going to do? How did this happen? I had just finished my first book, my autobiography, and it was ready to go to print. I had allowed the fears of being transparent and the lack of finances to keep me from releasing it for print. Fear will paralyze us from doing something and the stress from that fear caused my body to react. I was totally out of faith! I had to repent and make the adjustments in my life, and then I went immediately to the phone and released the book for printing. I could feel my back start to relax and healing start to come. I can't tell you I preached that conference pain free. I did not. I can tell you that as soon as God revealed to me I was in fear and I made the adjustments from fear to faith, relaxing came and the healing process started.

The fear didn't come all at once. It was a slow process of build up until I was consumed with it. I certainly had not fought the good fight of faith nor did I have my shield of faith in front of me. Our bodies are not designed to have tension and stress that come with fear, and my body rebelled against it. God is sovereign, but He acts on the principles of faith. Faith moves God because faith is in God. Fear moves Satan because fear is in Satan. What pleases God? Faith, and He will not move, apart from this.

Fear will cause me to be double-minded. Satan wants this, and he knows that faith will not work with double-mindedness. James 1:6-8 says, *Let him ask in faith, with no doubting, for he who doubts is like a wave of the sea driven and tossed by the wind. For let not that man suppose that he will receive anything from the Lord; he is a double-minded man, unstable in ALL his ways.* It says ALL, not some, of his ways. Being double-minded is jumping from one side to the other. Yes, I believe; no, I don't. Many Christians do this and that is exactly what I was doing when I would not release my first book for printing. I would go back and forth from faith in God's promise to supply all that was needed for the printing to fear that we would go in the hole on it. Satan had lured me into the trap of being double-minded.

Another way that Satan has gotten me into this trap is concerning our finances. It takes money to keep our bus going from place to place sharing the Gospel, and we have many wonderful people who partner with us in this ministry. Many times when things were tight, my mind would be double-minded. I would jump from faith and hope to doubt and fear that all the needs would be met.

When we put a letter in the post office we believe that it will reach its destination. We don't jump in a car and follow the post office vehicle to see if it gets to its destination. No! We believe that the post office employees will get the letter to the right address. How much greater are the promises of God than the post office? Any time we find ourselves moving back and forth, we are double-minded and unstable in all our ways. We will receive nothing from God. The thing that moves God is faith.

What are you believing for? See it through the eyes of faith. Find a promise from God for your situation and stand on it. No jumping back and forth. God's will is in His Word. Get in the Word, find the promise, and don't budge from it.

Fear is a force, the same as faith is a force. Fear will push us or faith will push us. If we ever allow the door of fear to open, we are in trouble. Satan wants to put fear on us. Every time my husband and I are going on the road for a long time, the enemy loves to put fear in our path. I have to look at that and say NO, you have tried it before and I was not given a spirit of fear, but of power, love and sound mind. If God is for me, who can be against me? We push fear out of the way, and rise up with faith words, speaking who we are in Christ and what Christ is in us, and know that He is going to lead us to people who need the light.

When we are in fear we are not in faith. We have to stand up, and know that we have deliverance from the power of Satan. How do we expect to feel when we stand before God and say, "Your Word is not true, it is not so, you did not tell me the truth." I was telling God I did not believe that He was able to supply what He said in His promises to me. When we walk in fear that is what we are saying. To remedy this situation, we must start confessing what His Word says, whether we feel like it is so in our life or not. Then it will become a reality in our lives. We must get our thinking in line with God's Word, then our believing will be right. When our believing is right, then we can confess, say, affirm, witness, and testify what God's Word says about us. This is when we will succeed, and life will become different.

Chapter 12
OTHER ENEMIES TO FAITH
**Enemies to our faith will stifle our
faith, if not pull us totally out of faith**

If we are to *live by faith and not by sight,* then faith is
as vital to our spiritual life as breath is to our
physical life. If we stop breathing we will
eventually die physically. If we stop living by faith
we will eventually die spiritually. Let's look at
some other enemies that will stifle our faith, if
not pull us totally out of faith.

**When we are presumptuous or self-willed
we are not in faith!** The Bible is very clear about
presumption, and it is an enemy to our faith. The
Psalmist cries out to God for a cleansing from
secret faults, and to keep him from
presumptuous sins (Psalm 19:12, 13). In 2 Peter
2:10 the Apostle speaks about the false teacher
being presumptuous. To live presumptuously is
to live a life that is marked by bold, excessive
self-confidence. It is an attitude that has its belief
supported by probability. A life of faith is marked
by God-confidence and faith that is based on the
facts of the Bible.

We have to be careful to stay out of presumption, and if the Holy Spirit reveals we have presumption in us, we must repent and move to faith based on the Bible facts. Philippians 3:3 ... *rejoice in Christ Jesus, and have NO confidence in the flesh.* To keep the enemy of presumption away we must have our confidence in the ability of God working through us, not on our own self-will and worldly ways.

A lack of knowledge of the Word of God is another enemy to our faith.

Hosea 4:6 says, *My people are destroyed for lack of knowledge.* Isaiah 5:13 says, *Therefore My people have gone into captivity, because they have no knowledge....* What we don't know can hurt us! This is important. We travel all over the United States and Canada, and even though we may not be aware of a traffic law in a certain place, we are still held accountable if we break it. Ignorance of the law is no excuse. It is the same with our journey through this life. We must know what are the laws for this journey. They are only found in God's Word. Key: Faith begins where the will of God is known. God's will is His word. How do we know God's will? We must go to God's book to find what His will is. Romans 10:17 says, *So then faith comes by hearing, and hearing by the word of*

God. No one has arrived yet. The Word is full of revelation and we must always be open and teachable. It is very dangerous to think that we know it all! This enemy to our faith is done away with by having a working knowledge of the Word of God!

Having a sense of unworthiness or a sense of sin consciousness is another enemy. We will stay in bondage with this kind of thinking. The enemy will pound on us. We have to let go of our past and forgive ourselves. We need a revelation of who we are in Christ. I have Christ in my life and I am not a SINNER. Romans 3:23 says, *for all have sinned and fall short of the glory of God.* The word "have" sinned is past tense. Jesus became my sin on the cross (2 Corinthians 5:21). That is the great exchange! He took my sin so I could have life. I am not a SINNER but a SAINT who sins. Big difference! I am now a new creation according to 2 Corinthians 5:17. It goes on to say all things have become new. How can that be? I still have the same past but the smell has been taken out of it because my life is now in Christ. I had to forgive myself for the past mistakes I made, not only to me, but also to my family. God forgave me my sins when I repented of them and He remembers them no more

(Jeremiah 31:34). When I don't forgive myself, I am not putting worth to the cross and saying that what Jesus did was not enough.

We all love gifts. This forgiveness is a gift to us and we don't merit it nor can we earn it. The gift of salvation is freely given to us. Jesus earned it for us. But by faith we must accept the gift. A sense of unworthiness or always looking at how I miss the mark (which is what sin means) produces a lack of confidence and assurance in the promises of God. We all have areas that we are still struggling with. This will always be true this side of heaven. We are being perfected daily into the image of Christ and when that last perfection comes, we go home! Our home is heaven if we are children of God. We must keep our eyes on Jesus and His Word and not on our imperfections. Be bold and know that boldness is not arrogance. The world needs us to go boldly into the throne room of God with our faith level high on their behalf. This enemy of our faith will go when the Jesus consciousness is raised.

Wrong words or negative words are very much enemies to our faith. We can't be complaining, lazy, or being inconsistent with our words. Remember Proverbs 6:2, *You are snared by the words of your mouth. You are taken by the words of* *your mouth.* Words are vital. This is covered in Chapter 15 "What is Coming Out of Our Mouth?" We keep this enemy away from our faith with right words!

A lack of understanding of our place in Him and of His place in us is a huge enemy. I believe this one is a key to all the other enemies of our faith. We need to study the book of Ephesians from time to time to keep reminded of our place in Jesus Christ. Chapters 1,2,3 of Ephesians is about our heavenly bank account: adoption, acceptance, redemption, forgiveness, wisdom, inheritance, the seal of the Holy Spirit, life, grace, citizenship, which in a nutshell is every spiritual blessing.

In chapters 4-6 we learn about our spiritual walk, which is rooted in our spiritual wealth. *For we are His workmanship, created in Christ Jesus for good works,...that we should walk in them* (Ephesians 2:10). We have riches beyond measure, but live as beggars! *Even when we were dead in trespasses, made us alive together with Christ (by grace you have been saved), and raised us up together and made us sit together in the heavenly places in Christ Jesus* (Ephesians 2:5,6). This is talking about our spiritual position in Christ! Right now we are raised together with Christ in His resurrection, together in His ascension, together in this present rule, and sitting together with Christ in the heavenly places with the enemy under our feet!

One day physically we will be with Christ, but now we have to understand that spiritually we are already positioned in Christ and Christ is in the heavenlies. With this heavenly position comes our spiritual resources (Ephesians 1:3), and Christ's authority over evil (1:19-23). We are to be declaring the eternal purposes of God to the enemy (3:9-11). Knowing our position in Christ will keep the enemy under our feet, not us under his feet!

Chapter 13
NATURAL FAITH OR SUPERNATURAL GOD-FAITH?
**My hope will see it, my faith will
stand for it, and God will bring it in**

There are different kinds of faith. One is of the head and the other is of the heart. Natural faith or worldly faith believes that an oncoming car is going to stay on his side of the road, or that a chair will hold us up. When we come to a crosswalk, we cross on a green light expecting the cars with the red light to stop. When traveling across a bridge, we don't inspect the structure, although on some bridges it would be wise. No! We just proceed across the bridge and believe that we will get to the other side. Most people have that kind of faith. Supernatural faith is a gift from God. God-faith has confidence that even though I don't see something, even with every circumstance coming against me, I know that God's Word is true and that He will bring it about. My hope will see it, my faith will stand for it, and God will bring it in.

Proverbs 3:5 says, *Trust the Lord with all your heart (or spirit), and lean NOT on your own understanding (which is the mind, will and emotions).* This verse is one of the biggest keys we can have. A key opens and closes something. Natural faith trusts in what we see, hear, smell, touch, or feel. Our own understanding is our own mental process, our own human thinking. Supernatural God-faith trusts with the heart, not the head. ... *and does not doubt in his heart* (Mark 11:23). We are a spirit, we have a soul (mind, will, emotion), and we live in a body (1 Thessalonians 5:23). In Hebrews 4:12 it also tells us the Word of God is powerful to divide the spirit, soul, and body. This shows us that we live in three realms—We contact the spiritual realm with our spirit. We contact the intellectual realm with our soul, and we contact the physical realm with our physical body. Our body is simply our earth suit, which we need to complete our journey through this life.

To move from natural faith to supernatural God-faith we have to know the difference between what our heart is saying to us and what our head is saying to us. We can have faith in our heart and not have faith in our head. Faith of the heart is only moved by what the Word of God says, not by what people or the circumstances say. Our own understanding of the situation will not help us, but only by trusting in the understanding that comes from the Word of God. We need to trust in the Lord with all our heart, and not trust in our five senses, our understanding, or our intelligence. Don't put faith in the world. I only put my faith in what the Word of God says!

Abraham and Sarah had faith that believed in spite of the circumstances. I am sure their heads tried to confuse them on the promise that God had given to them. But they did not lean to their own understanding which I am sure was telling them, NO way can this promise come forth. Don't you know how old you are? Thomas, on the other hand, had faith that saw only with the natural eye. His faith had to touch the wounds in Jesus' side before he would believe. He had been a disciple of Jesus for a little over three years and heard all that was taught and promised, but still would not go beyond his natural thinking of having to see first to believe that Jesus had risen from the grave. Jesus understood this and told him that he believed because he saw, but BLESSED are the ones who have not seen but still believe.

The world told me that my son was going to

stay on drugs, but Scripture told me in Isaiah 54:13, *Great shall be the peace of my children.* So I prayed according to Scripture. If my child was going to have great peace, then I knew he would be freed from drugs because he had no peace on drugs. So he had to get in God's will to have peace. And again, Acts 16:31 says, ... *believe on the Lord Jesus Christ, and you will be saved,* **and your household.** My part was to believe (rely on, trust in, have confidence in). It was more than mental assent. I believed in the Lord Jesus Christ so I knew that my household would be saved. God's part was to save. I stood on those promises. Know what you are praying for. If we don't know what we want from God, we will not receive it. Our mind will give us a battle every time.

I hear people say all the time, "If I don't see it, I won't believe it." These people are earth bound. They are not basing their faith on God and His Word, but on the world and its ways. As children of God we cannot put our faith in worldly ways or worldly thinking. There are many Scriptures telling us *that if we are friends with the world it makes us an enemy with God* (James 4:4), *we are not to be conformed to the world* (Romans 12:2), *we are to remain unspotted from the world* (James 1:27), *that the world is passing away* (1 John 2:17), and the Scriptures go on and on. We are children of God and the Word says …*because as He is, so are we in this world* (1 John 4:17). We need to catch that, as He is, so are we! We are in this world, but once we are children of God, we are no longer OF it. If we are not of it, we should not think we could get our help from it. Our help comes from the Lord! Our help will come ONLY from the Lord. We belong to the unseen realm of God, which only operates by supernatural GOD-FAITH! We must not only *live by faith and not sight,* but we must *WALK by faith, not by sight* (2 Corinthians 5:7).

At one time I had a huge problem with my neck that was called "degenerating disc disease." I had just come through a huge trauma in my life when I started to experience pain in my back and hand with my fingers going numb. I was a manicurist at the time and my hands were money to me. I could hardly hold a fingernail file. I went to the doctor and had a test to see what was wrong. I was told that it could not be cured but would be maintained with treatment. I was also told that it would worsen in time. I needed supernatural God-faith to get me through that rough spot in my life. To get supernatural God-faith I went to God's Word and found the Scripture in 2 Corinthians 4:18 ... *we do not look at the things which are seen, but at the things which are not seen....* This means that I am not to look at my condition the way the world would look at it but the way God says it is. I started looking up healing Scriptures to build my faith in the unseen. My supernatural, God-given faith. The Lord did show me areas that I had to correct in my working conditions, like cut down on the hours! I needed to take more frequent breaks to walk around and allow my body to move. I also needed to live and walk by faith with our finances! Trust my heavenly Father! I made a commitment to adjust my life and then I went to find someone to agree with me in prayer.

We can go to prayer by ourselves but when we have someone agreeing with us in prayer, there is twice as much power! Notice I said "agree" with me. I wanted total healing with no operation! When two people agree in prayer they need to do just that–agree! What is the faith level of the person being prayed for, and what is the faith level of the person praying? *If our faith can grow, then it can be big or small.* I did not want someone praying with me who believed that my problem could only be solved by an operation, when I was praying and believing for total healing without an operation.

Mark 6:5-6 tells us, *Now He could do not mighty work there, except that He laid His hands on a FEW SICK PEOPLE AND HEALED THEM. And He marveled because of their UNBELIEF. Then He went about the villages in a circuit, teaching.* Not everybody was healed by Jesus. Was it His fault? Of course not. It was a lack of belief. His faith did not override the faith of someone else and neither will ours.

When I am praying for someone I find out what they are believing God for and I agree with them. We all have to start where we are and work our way forward with our supernatural God-given faith. I always try to find a point of agreement. Sometimes we need to stop and do some teaching on faith before we pray. Sometimes we have to do something in the natural realm before we can ask for something out of the supernatural realm. An example would be agreeing with someone about finances. If they don't work or look for work and just sleep all day, I certainly would not agree with them for finances to come. I need to teach them about the financial plan of God found in the Bible. Then I would agree with them. Their darkness about that subject has been enlightened.

Healing is the same! I believe it is the will of God to heal and that Jesus paid the price for our healing. If someone believes the teaching that they will be healed "IF" it is the will of God, then they need teaching on what the will of God **is** concerning healing. Why would our heavenly Father want us sick? He doesn't!

It is the Word of God that opens the heart and brings us from natural faith to supernatural God-faith. We need to be sensitive to where people are and what they want from God, not what we want for them. I feel that is why a lot of prayers are not answered because there is no agreement. Many people just pray confusing prayers that don't go higher than the ceiling. We can't go against Scripture and get prayer answered. We must base all our prayers on the will of God, which is His Word. I have heard it said, "Our attitude will determine our altitude." The healing in my neck did not come overnight! I knew the key to my healing was having a positive attitude. This kept my faith level high. I knew I needed to keep exercising my faith by thanking, praising, and believing God for my healing. I didn't care how I felt when I started my day; *I continued to look at the things which were not seen.* Then one day the healing came totally! We can never forget that heart-faith is supernatural God-faith!

Chapter 14
THE GREATEST MOUNTAIN TO OVERCOME
**We cannot walk in love and
unforgiveness at the same time**

Jesus tells us we *can* move mountains. He gives us a powerful lesson in Mark 11:22-24.

Have faith in God. For assuredly, I say to you, whoever says to this mountain, "Be removed and be cast into the sea," and does not doubt in his heart, but believes that those things he says will be done, he will have whatever he says. Therefore I say to you, whatever things you ask when you pray, believe that you receive them, and you will have them.

However, in the next breath, He tells us what can hinder these mountains from moving.

Whenever you stand praying, if you have anything against anyone, forgive him, that your Father in heaven may also forgive you your trespasses. But if you DO NOT forgive, neither will your Father in heaven forgive your trespasses (Mark 11:25).

Forgiveness! People say to me, "But you don't know what he/she did to me. How can I forgive him for what he has done?" Well, you can and you must forgive him or her if you want to grow in your Christian walk. It is an act of the will. Jesus said to do it, so it is possible. We cannot hold unforgiveness and walk in love at the same time. Jesus doesn't say to forgive others if we want to. No! It is a command given to us by Jesus. I want forgiveness so I MUST GIVE forgiveness.

Jesus is saying unforgiveness is the greatest mountain that has to be removed before we can do anything else. If your prayers are not being answered or your faith doesn't seem to be "working," ask yourself, "Do I have anything against anyone? Do I need to go and speak with them?" I always ask the Holy Spirit to show me if I have unforgiveness in my heart. This was a key to my walk of faith I learned very quickly. Galatians 5:6 says, ...*but faith working through love.* I do not hold on to unforgiveness because I know that the only way supernatural God-faith will work is by love. If we have a flashlight and we do not put batteries in it or the batteries have lost their power, it will not work. The flashlight has power because of the batteries. That is like our faith. Love is the battery in our flashlight of faith. Love causes my faith to work. If I have unforgiveness, I do not have love. If I have no love then I have no faith! Curse dead works and get rid of it.

In the verses right around Mark 11:25 on unforgiveness, the apostles thought they needed more faith in order to forgive, so they said to the Lord, *Increase our faith* (Luke 17:5). Remember, they were tax collectors, fishermen, rough people. The Lord said, *"If you have faith as a mustard seed, you can say to this mulberry tree, be pulled up by the roots and be planted in the sea, and it would obey you"* (Luke 17:6). The mustard seed is a very small seed, but it knows what it is and how big it shall grow. The mustard seed knows its destiny. Likewise, we must know our destiny. We must understand our authority and know God's power, His will, His provision, and His purposes. That seed becomes a plant. The power of life surges into the tender young plant in such a great extent that even a mountain of earth cannot stop it from pushing upward. That is what our faith is like.

I love to garden and grow vegetables and flowers. I like to start the plants myself so I start with a tiny seed. It is a very tiny seed and I put a lot of dirt over it, but it will grow anyway. It is nourished, it gets cared for, and with the right temperature and the right condition, it will grow.

To me this is an amazing thing that one little seed can produce a huge plant that will produce a huge amount of whatever it is. Just like our faith. It will push up through the entire dirt that is thrown upon it if the conditions are right, and one of the conditions God says we must have is forgiveness. We must totally forgive. Unforgiveness will STOP US.

Chapter 15
WHAT IS COMING OUT OF OUR MOUTH?
A confession that glorifies the devil is an unconscious declaration that God is a failure

Confession is another word for profession–what we profess to believe is what comes out of our mouth. Hebrews 4:14 says, *Seeing then that we have a great High Priest who has passed through the heavens, Jesus the Son of God, let us hold fast our confession.* Hold fast means saying the same thing over and over. No matter what, hold fast; do not be double-minded. To lay hold or take hold of our confession means we use, strengthen, seize, or keep with vigor and power. What is our confession? What is coming out of our mouth? The confession of our lips will give either God or Satan dominion over us. Is our confession that Jesus Christ is our Savior and Lord?

Taking hold of what we believe in daily life is a process. We can beg and cry and still be defeated. These are strong words, but if we don't believe for anything, we won't get anything. If we don't believe, even if we are in the perfect will of God, we will still be defeated. We must believe. Remember, believe means to trust in and be fully convinced of. We have to appropriate what belongs to us. Hebrews 11:6 says, *But without faith, it is impossible to please Him, for he who comes to God must believe that He is, and that He is a rewarder of those who diligently seek Him.*

The Gospel of Mark records that one synagogue leader's daughter was very sick and not expected to live. But her father, Jairus, had faith that Jesus could heal her so he asked, or rather begged, Jesus to *come and lay Your hands on her, that she may be healed, and she will live* (Mark 5:23). Jairus didn't waiver in his faith. He didn't say *maybe* she will be healed if you come– no. He said, "She *will* be healed." He spoke prophetically over his daughter.

People close to Jairus tried to get him to think logically and use some common sense. They said, *"Your daughter is dead. Why trouble the teacher any further?"* (Mark 5:35) Jesus heard this and spoke faith words to Jairus. *"Do not be afraid, only believe."* In other words, "Don't listen to the report in the natural, Jairus. You've already said that if I come and lay my hands on your daughter, she will be healed and she will live. So do not be afraid, only believe, only trust."

This same Jesus is here today. Hebrews 13:8 says, *Jesus Christ is the same yesterday, today, and forever.* He says to you and me, "Do not be afraid. Only believe." Stick with your confession and don't look at the natural, don't look at what people are saying, just hang in there with Him and go on. Then in verse 37 of Mark 5, Jesus *permitted no one to follow Him except Peter, James, and John, the brother of James.* Faith people were all He allowed to go with Him.

Then Jesus went to Jairus' house and saw people weeping and wailing loudly. The mourners were there. When He came in, He said to them, *"Why make this commotion and weep? The child is not dead, but sleeping."* Jesus spoke prophetically, saying that she was coming out of that death. The mourners made fun of Him. Anytime we stand in faith, beyond the natural, beyond what people believe can happen, we are going to be ridiculed. People do not understand people of faith and the enemy will send them right in. What they are after is our faith and a great way to do that is to ridicule. They ridiculed Jesus and they are going to ridicule us for our faith. But notice what He did. All those who ridiculed, all those who were not in belief, He put them outside. Put them outside of your life. Don't allow them to be within where you are standing in faith. Jesus took the parents of the child and those who were with Him and entered where the child was lying (V 40). He spoke to her and the little girl immediately came alive and He said, *"Give her something to eat."*

We are always going to have people who come against us. Do it the way Jesus did it. He only allowed the people of faith, the ones who would stand in faith, to be with Him.

After we purchased our greyhound bus, my husband spent a whole year on his off time transforming the inside into a beautiful home with custom oak furnishings throughout. Then when it was time to do the bodywork on the outside and paint it, all hell broke loose. We had driven the bus into the middle of the field of some friends. We masked it off, like you mask to paint a car before painting. This 35-foot bus was about three cars worth of masking. Just as we finished the masking, the weather turned. Suddenly the sky became dark and the wind began to blow hard. It looked like it was going to rain. In the natural, it looked like there was no way that the masking papers were going to stay on. We had just spent days getting it prepared to paint. Days. But the intercessors and I prayed to God. My husband and I stood in faith. We knew God could change the weather on our behalf. And I prayed, "Father, don't allow anyone to come out here who is not standing in faith." We did not want anyone around us who would speak negative words, or speak against what we knew God was going to do. Then we watched God hold the weather. Did it rain? Yes, just enough to keep the dust down, so the dust would not get in the paint. God used the storm for our good.

If there is a right confession, the opposite must also be true. What is wrong confession? It is confession of defeat, failure, and the supremacy of Satan. Talking about how the devil is keeping us from success, holding us in bondage, or keeping us sick is the confession of defeat. Such a confession simply glorifies the devil. Confession is witnessing to the truth that we embrace. It is testifying of something we know and confirming something we believe. Let's make sure that what is coming out of our mouth does not glorify the devil, but that it witnesses to what God's Word says about a matter.

We overcome by the word of our testimony (Revelation 12:11). When we testify to what God has done for us, it will make us overcome. By the same token, when we testify to what the devil is doing and list our failures and defeats, we are glorifying the devil. That is not going to make us overcome, nor will it make anybody else overcome. Many people lose the blessing that God has for them simply because of their words. They are defeated and life becomes a grind for them.

Actually, a confession that glorifies the devil is an unconscious declaration that God is a failure. Wow! Such a confession destroys our faith and holds us in bondage. When we are saved we confess the Lordship of Jesus. He begins to have dominion over us and rules in our life; on the other hand, when we confess Satan's ability to hinder us and keep us from success even if we are a Christian, we are giving Satan dominion over us. He is the god of this world and he will move right in because we permit him to do so. Even though it might be a permission of ignorance, or unconscious consent, it is nevertheless consent. When Satan has dominion, we are filled with weakness and fear.

So let's stop confessing doubt and start confessing faith. We need to start talking about who we are and what we are in Christ. We are believers! *We are a new creation* (2 Corinthians

5:17). We need to believe that, and think that.
...*submit to God. Resist the devil and he will flee from
you* (James 4:7). First submit, then resist. In the
name of Jesus Christ, refuse to doubt, and doubt
will leave us. Instead of confessing doubt and
fear, let's confess God's Word, and what it says.
Fear not, for I am with you (Isaiah 41:10). Therefore
you can say, I am a child of God and He is with
me. *For God has not given us a spirit of fear, but of
power, and of love, and of a sound mind* (2 Timothy
1:7). I am not a doubter. I am a believer. We need
to stop talking the devil's language of doubt and
fear. Start talking God's language of faith.

His Word declares that *by His stripes we were
healed* (1 Peter 2:24). Matthew 8:17 says, *That it
might be fulfilled which was spoken by Isaiah the prophet,
saying: He Himself took our infirmities and bore our
sickness.* Instead of confessing that Jesus took our
infirmities and bore our sickness, we declare we
still have them and we will remain sick. When we
start speaking that He already took it for us, we
will receive our healing. Too often we receive the
testimony of our natural senses instead of the
testimony of God's Word. We will walk across
a busy street when the light is green with the
confidence that the cars with the red light will
stop and stay stopped until we get across the

street. We don't know anything about the people in those cars, yet we trust that they will keep their foot on the brake until the light turns green or we get to the other side. We have a Lord and Savior who took our pain and shame to give us eternal life with all its benefits and we still don't trust Him to see us through hard times.

Proverbs 3:5 says, *Trust in the Lord with all your heart (not your head) and lean NOT on your own understanding.* This is one of the BIGGEST keys we will ever have. This is also one of the biggest challenges to our confession. Supernatural God-faith is of the heart. Whatever is in your heart will come out your mouth.

When Mary received the report from the angel that she was going to have a Son and His name would be called Jesus, she asked, *"How can this be, since I do not know a man?"* She didn't ask this question doubting it could be done, but how will it be done. There is a big difference between the two. The angel told her that the Holy Spirit would come upon her, and the power of the Highest would overshadow her. The Child to be born was also to be called the Son of God. Take a moment and think about her situation. She was a teenager, engaged to be married. I am sure her mind was racing about what the repercussions would be to all of this (death by stoning!) and what her husband to be, Joseph, would do. She certainly needed supernatural God-faith to bring all this about! All the odds were against her. She was going to bring into the world the Messiah! Who would believe all of this? She was told that God is the God of the impossible. Her confession was, *"Let it be to me according to your word"* (Luke 1:28-38). Jesus came into this world through the supernatural God-faith of a young woman and this must teach us something. *We* must practice God's Word. Remember, when we get a report that is against the Word of God or looks impossible to us, we need to take the Word of God and confess into the atmosphere what God says the outcome will be! Allow God to give us the diagnosis and the prognosis from His Word, not what the world says the outcome will be.

Get rid of things that want you to agree with the circumstances, instead of with the Word of God. We are used to our circumstances and they try to dictate our life. We go to the doctor and we believe him. We believe what our checkbook says, what our parents have said about us, or what our boss may say about us. We believe those things instead of what God says. Don't do that. I don't believe anything that is negative. Right thoughts produce right words, and right words produce right action! The Bible says that we are to find Scripture and stand on it. How long? As long as it takes. When we've done all we know to do, then stand, believing God's Word is true!

Chapter 16
FAITH THEN AND NOW
God will use our nothing to provide something if we will believe that he can and will

We can learn much about faith from the lives of people recorded in the Bible. The desperation of one woman and her faith are recorded in 2 Kings 4:1-7: *(author's overview)*

The woman in this Scripture is just called a certain woman who was the wife of a prophet who worked with and served the prophet Elisha. Her husband died and she called on the man of God for some answers to her dilemma. She is left with no money to pay the creditors and they are coming to take her sons and make them slaves. Her sons are all she has left. She speaks to Elisha about her husband. She does not talk about what a wonderful prophet, husband, or dad he has been, but says to Elisha *...and you know he FEARED the Lord.*

Fearing the Lord means that a person has knowledge of God's laws and obeys them. When we say that we have the fear of the Lord, it reflects a life-style which always takes into account that there is an all-wise, all-powerful, all-righteous God who holds people accountable for their actions. To act sinfully is to act as though God is too weak, too ignorant, or too inconsistent to enforce His will. To live in loving fellowship with God is possible only to those who fear Him. To say that her husband "Feared the Lord" were the right words to activate the promises of God. She is saying, okay Elisha, you know all this. Now I need some help. This woman is feeling very alone and desperate. She needs a miracle and knows that she has grounds to ask for one.

She is asked what she has in the house. She had nothing but a jar of oil. God will use our nothing to provide something if we will believe that he can and will. Elisha told her to go and get empty vessels from her neighbors, as many as she could. He gave exact instructions saying, *"Do not gather a few."* We can assume that her husband must have helped his neighbors whenever they needed help. Because Elisha told her to gather many vessels would have to mean that they would give them to her. It is obvious that in past times her husband had sown abundant help into his neighbors' lives and now he would reap abundant help back for his family. God used those neighbors to meet the need of his family, even after he was dead. She had the Word of God to stand on.

This woman did exactly what the prophet told her to do. After she gathered the vessels, they were filled with oil, and she could pay off her debt. She believed and she obeyed. And notice that Elisha said, "Don't gather a few." That's a big key. Look for big things; see your God big. See the answer instead of the problem or circumstances. Believe the Word of the Lord and what it says.

We can learn from the example of another woman of great faith recorded in 2 Kings 4:8-37: *(author's overview)*

This woman is called a notable or wealthy woman. She and her husband had money. In the Scripture it says that Elisha would pass by often and they would feed him. She begins to notice this pattern and asked her husband to fix a room upstairs for him. They put in it all the things the man of God would need to be comfortable. She and her husband wanted to take care of the man of God. It is important to take care of the men and women of God who are spending their lives seeking God and serving God on our behalf.

They are not only taking care of Elisha but he has his servant Gehazi with him. Elisha must have known the king and commander of the army at that time because he had his servant ask if he could speak to them on the couple's behalf. They were told by the woman that they needed no help in that area, but he did find out that they had no children. Her husband was old it says. They had no son to carry on the family name and Elisha told her, *"About this time next year you shall embrace a son." And she said, "No, my lord, Man of God, do not lie to your maidservant!"* (4:16) She was saying, don't get my hopes up. I have waited a long time for a child! Don't say it if you don't mean it!

Just as Elisha had said, she bore a son at the appointed time Elisha had stated. What an exciting time it must have been in her household. After all those years of hoping, now she has a son. Her husband was old so they both had to have had faith and not doubt in their hearts to bring that word forth. They would have to put down the worldly report that said her husband was too old. They stood in supernatural God-faith and brought forth the promise of God, a son.

This happy event turns to darkness when the

son gets older. He is working in the fields with his father when he says, "*...My head, My head*" (4:19). Farming in those days was hard, hot work, and I believe the boy had a sunstroke. They took the boy to his mother where he sat on her lap until noon and then he died. As a mother, I can't even imagine the emotion she had to deal with. She takes her dead child upstairs and lays him on the bed of the man of God, which represents taking him to God. She leaves him there, goes to her husband and says to bring her a donkey. She is going to find the man of God and bring him back. Her husband is confused because it is neither the Sabbath nor a church day, so why is she going to church? She didn't tell him their son had died. All she said was "It is well."

It even says she saddled her own donkey. I don't know if I could have done that if my son had just died. I find it interesting that she saddled the donkey, but her servant did the driving. In her emotional state she knew what she could do and what she couldn't do. This is very important! She set her face like flint, and she knew that the man of God could bring her child back to life. She could not be stopped and she did not stop to talk to any one. She was going as fast as she could to the man of God. She did not speak one negative word against what she knew in her heart could happen. Elisha saw her coming and sent his servant to ask her *"...Is it well with you? Is it well with your husband? Is it well with the child?" And she answered, "It is well"* (4:26). That's all she said. Not another word.

When she got to the man of God she grabbed hold of him and would not let go. Elisha's servant comes to handle the situation by removing her. Elisha said, "Leave her alone. She is in deep distress." The Lord did not show him what the distress was and this shows us that prophets are not shown everything all the time. She puts the pressure on Elisha by telling him that she had not asked for a son and she had told the prophet that in the beginning. Elisha told his servant to get ready to travel and lay the prophet's staff on the face of the child. This was preparation for the miracle.

In the midst of the trials and tribulations, in the midst of the circumstances, don't stop to talk about it. Don't stop to have people agree with you in the midst of the turmoil. The only thing you want to agree with is the Word of God. We do not want anyone to pat us on the back and say, "Oh poor you, it's OK to feel that way." It's not OK to feel that way. Run as fast as you can to God and His Word.

This mother is not going to be put off and she is not going to accept just the servant going to her son. She wants the man of God and is not going to leave until he comes. The son she had waited all those years for was now dead. But she knows the man who knows the God who gave her this son. This is the way we need to be about God. We need to accept nothing but His presence. The servant went ahead and the woman followed WITH Elisha. The servant placed the staff on the boy but the boy did not awaken. *When Elisha came into the house, there was the child, lying dead on his bed. He went in therefore, shut the door behind the two of them, and prayed to the Lord* (4:32,33).

Now notice he shut the door and he prayed. The only way we are going to get God's direction is in prayer. Elisha got alone with God in prayer! The only way to get built up in our faith is to get alone with God. No one could give him the answers he needed but God and God alone. He had to know the covenant promises of God for this situation. He needed faith of the heart or supernatural God-faith to raise this child up. He knew this son had been given to this couple by a miracle of God. He also knew that it would take another miracle to bring this child back from the dead. He knew it was the hand of Satan who had taken this boy from this family, but he also knew that the hand of God would bring him back. Elisha wanted to know what God wanted done in the midst of the situation. I believe he was asking God, "How do I pray? How do I raise this child?" When Elisha got his orders or direction from God, his faith level went to a supernatural God-faith level because that is what it would take to raise him from the dead. He was fully assured that God would do it!

And he went up and lay on the child, and put his mouth on his mouth, his eyes on his eyes, and his hands on his hands; and he stretched himself out on the child, and the flesh of the child became warm (2Kings:4:34). Elisha received direction from God on what would work to raise the boy from the dead. God will show us what will work in our circumstances. We read in the rest of the verses of this Bible account that the boy sneezed seven times and he awoke and he was taken to his mother.

Many times in the midst of circumstances, we need to say, "It is well." These are faith words. This mother was a normal human being with emotions. She was cringing inside. Can you imagine what it was like to drive fifteen to twenty miles by donkey with her son dead and her mind in such turmoil? But she did not let go of her faith. She did not believe what her head said; she kept going, and that is exactly what we need to do. Don't believe the bad report; just stay focused on Jesus.

We can learn from both of these women how to take a horrible situation and turn our faith from "natural" to "supernatural, God-faith." Supernatural God-faith worked for them then and it will work for us now!

Chapter 17
THE POWER OF
A RENEWED MIND
**A renewed mind turns anger
into joy and doubt into faith**

The Bible is the Word of God and contains
God's thoughts. Of course God's thoughts are
different from man's thoughts. As we study
God's Word and know His thoughts, can we
dare to think God's thoughts? He has told us,
*"For My thoughts are not your thoughts, Nor are your
ways My ways," says the Lord. "For as the heavens are
higher than the earth, so are My ways higher than your
ways, and My thoughts than your thoughts"* (Isaiah
55:8,9). Yes, we can think His thoughts, but only
after we get our thinking in line with His Word.

*Each one is tempted when he is drawn away by his own
desires and enticed. Then when desire has conceived, it
gives birth to sin; and sin, when it is full-grown, brings
forth death. Do not be deceived...*(James 1:14-16).
DON'T BE DECEIVED or tricked! The word
"desire" in these verses is the same word for lust
(*epithumia*) in the Greek. This is an active and

individual desire resulting from the diseased condition of the soul (mind, will, emotions). Any part of our soul realm which is not renewed by the Word of God is diseased. We can then be drawn away from God's purposes and the devil will entice us in those diseased areas of our soul realm. If we do not allow those diseased areas to be cured by the renewing of our mind, we will keep sliding downhill even to a point of death. Don't be deceived! Renewing the mind, is the only cure for disease in the soul realm. The cause of this disease? The fall of man in the Garden of Eden.

We know that our words can be uplifting or damaging. In a sense, our words create. That is why it's so important for our minds to be renewed daily. What is in our hearts comes out of our mouth. When our mind is renewed, we have right thinking, and that right thinking comes out of our mouth. I believe that Romans 12:1-2 is the hinge of the New Testament:

I beseech you therefore, brethren, by the mercies of God, that you present your bodies a living sacrifice, holy, acceptable to God, which is your reasonable service. And do not be conformed to this world, but be transformed by the renewing of your mind, that you may prove what is that good and acceptable and perfect will of God.

Everything hinges on a renewed mind—our words, our conduct, and our attitude. What does it mean to not be conformed to this world? It means don't act or look like the world. We are in the world but not of it any more if we are children of God. We are to look and act different from the world. It is sad to say, but conformity to the world is coming inside the church. Who is the church? The people of God! People tell me all the time, "This is the Twenty-First Century, Judy. Get with it." I am with it and I shall not be conformed to this world because this world is passing away and those conformed to it will go with it. Don't be deceived!

To be transformed means that we respond to things differently than we did before. Something will go into a transformer and come out different than how it went in. That is how it should be with us. When I became a child of God my spirit became alive to God, but my soul (mind, will, emotions) was the same with the same old "stinking thinking."

I am now in the kingdom of God and must have kingdom thinking which will only come from the kingdom manual, the Bible. There is no short cut and no other way but to get into the Bible and allow the Holy Spirit to renew my mind. I am no longer moved by the things of the world or what the world tries to dictate to me. To the child of God it is not fashionable to THINK, LOOK, or ACT like the world.

A renewed mind turns anger into joy and doubt into faith. As we renew our mind, faith words that we speak begin to erase the old things that we have computed. Now we have a renewed tape going into our mind. We open our mouth and faith comes out. We learn to see everything from a new perspective–our heavenly Father's.

If our believing is wrong, it is because our thinking is wrong, and if our thinking is wrong, it is because our mind has not been renewed with the Word of God. Sometimes the teaching of the Word of God will not seem reasonable to the natural man, because his or her mind has not been renewed by the Word. We will only have supernatural God-faith when we get busy and renew our mind with the Word of God. Remember, this is the only cure for a diseased soul realm.

So how important is renewing our mind? I would say VERY!

Chapter 18
SHOW THEM NO MERCY
Evil spirits do not know what you are thinking; they will only respond to speaking

Here in the United States we are used to a democracy. God does not have a democracy but a Theocracy–He is Lord and Creator of all. We call him Lord, which means supreme controller; then we go out and do exactly as we want. We have become tolerant of evil in our lives and lifestyle. The vertical bond with God should reflect in our horizontal social relationships! To live the life of supernatural God-faith we must have Jesus Christ as the supreme controller of our life. Who is in that vertical bond with us? Our purpose is to know God. Supernatural God-faith only comes from a vertical bond with God.

God brought the children of Israel out of Egypt supernaturally. They left with their enemy providing for their journey to the promise land. They left with a slave mentality, which would have to be changed to a conquering mentality for them to accomplish the purposes of God for their life. From the very beginning of their journey out of captivity, they would need a greater faith than natural faith. They would have to develop supernatural God-faith to survive this journey. They were given instructions during the journey the same as we are. Did they believe and follow? No! Only Joshua and Caleb went to the promise land. Everyone else over twenty years old died in the wilderness. Why did Joshua and Caleb get to go into the promise land? Because they had supernatural God-faith that, after spying out the land, they saw giants but brought back the report, *"Let us go up at once and take possession, for we are well able to overcome it"* (Numbers 13:30). All the others couldn't get past the giants they saw and said, *"We are like grasshoppers in our own eyes"* (Numbers 13:33).

Only those who were twenty years of age and younger were going into the promise land. Those were the ones who had and would become the victor and not the victim. They were going to a good land, a land that was large and flowing with milk and honey. In other words all they needed would be supplied for them in this land. The only thing they needed to know was that there were enemies to drive out of the land before they could occupy it. God warned the nation of Israel about their enemies before they approached the promise land. I believe He is still warning us today about the same enemies.

When we read the Bible there is a law of double reference—a natural application and a spiritual application. It was for the times it was written and it is for us now. I want us to take the natural and look at it in the spiritual.

We find keys to our walk of faith in Deuteronomy 7:1, 2:

When the Lord your God brings you into the land which you go to possess, and has cast out many nations before you, the Hittites and the Girgashites and the Amorites and the Canaanites and the Perizzites and the Hivites and the Jebusites, seven nations greater and mightier than you, and when the Lord your God delivers them OVER TO YOU, you shall conquer them and UTTERLY destroy them. You shall make no covenant with them, nor SHOW MERCY TO THEM.

Israel had to conquer these great nations in the natural before they could go into the land given to them by God. We have a spiritual application in these Scriptures. God is telling us that we will have to conquer these nations in our own lives before we can receive the purposes that He has for us. We are told to UTTERLY destroy them and make no covenant with them and show them no mercy. Romans 8:37 says, *Yet in all things we are more than conquerors through Him who loved us.* Jesus is the conqueror and we are more than conquerors. He won the war on the cross of Calvary for us but until we get to heaven, we will go through battles. Many are losing the battle. Jesus says in Mark 11:23, "...*whoever says to this mountain, Be removed and be cast into the sea, and does not doubt in his heart, but believes that those things he says will be done, he will have whatever he says.*" I believe spiritually, these nations are some of the mountains in our lives that must come down. I looked up the names of these nations in J.B. Jackson's book *A Dictionary of Scripture Proper Names.* Let's look at them one by one, and then speak to and take authority over these mountains one by one! Allow the Holy Spirit to shine a light in the dark areas of your life to bring adjustment and change. God is saying, "Where are you?" Be honest because He already knows.

HITTITES. The name means terror. Terror and fear go hand in hand which can cause panic. Everywhere I go I see people who are bound by terror and fear. This is a spiritual influence that will cause a stronghold in our life if we do not conquer it. I talked about fear in Chapter 11, *One*

Enemy to Faith–Fear. The only fear we are to have is the fear of the Lord. I had to conquer this in my own life. I had a great fear of snakes. Vic and I do a lot of mission work with a Bible camp in Wyoming. They have snakes. I could have allowed this fear and panic to stop me from being obedient to the call of God. When I am traveling around I find many people who are struggling with some kind of fear or panic that is keeping them bound. Some are so bound that they don't even drive anymore. *God has not given us a spirit of fear, but of power, love and a sound mind* (2 Timothy 1:7). From this verse we are told that fear is not of God. It says that when fear comes, it is a spirit that is demonic! Any spirit that is not of God is demonic! Joshua was told four times before he entered the promise land that he was to be **strong and courageous.** God tells us to speak and take authority over the spirit of fear and allow the Holy Spirit to fill our lives with **strength and courage.**

GIRGASHITES. The name means dwelling on clay soil. Webster's dictionary says that clay is a plastic earthly material. It can be molded into different forms. It is changeable! Isn't that what being double-minded is? Going from earthly thoughts to heavenly thoughts. This is covered more in Chapter 11, *One Enemy to Faith—Fear.* We have times in our life when we are double-minded. Many people with habits are on a cycle of recovery. They are always recovering from something. John 8:36 says, *Therefore if the Son makes you free, you shall be free indeed.* If we have been set free, the only way to stay free is by reading the Word of God, praying, and giving God thanks for keeping us free! I call this replacing a habit with a habit. We can't be going from doubt to faith and back to doubt all the time. *...he is a double-minded man, unstable in all his ways* (James 1:8). The Word is either true or it is not. To be double-minded is to have two ways of thinking! What a sobering thought! We need to fill our life with **stability**. Speak and take authority over this demonic influence of double-mindedness. Allow the Holy Spirit to **stabilize** our thinking patterns.

AMORITE. The name means sayer. They were people who dwelled on the summit of the mountains. How about PRIDE? Pride means that which is self-confident and boasting. Lucifer was the most beautiful of all angels and held a high position in heaven. He had it all going for him, but he started to think he did not need his Creator. The account of this is found in Isaiah

Chapter 14. Isaiah tells us the five "I wills " that caused Lucifer to not only lose his position in heaven but have his name changed to Satan. He had a lot of influence because not only was he cast out of heaven, one-third of the angels followed in his pride. Unfortunately, when pride is in our life it affects those around us. The problem in the Garden of Eden was that Adam and Eve went from God-dependency to self-dependency. Pride says, "I can do it myself, I don't need God." Pride is hung up on the I's— me, mine, and self-righteousness. If I have trouble looking someone in the eye and taking responsibility for what I have done by saying "I AM SORRY," I have pride in my life. Let's speak and take authority over the spiritual influence of pride. Allow the Holy Spirit to fill our life with **humility.**

CANAANITES. The name means zealous trafficker. They were people of commerce and very good merchants. I think this represents materialism, pleasure seeking, or worldly goods. We cannot be more zealous with worldly goods than we are with God's goods. I see people all the time being driven by work and making money. Why? So they can have more things. The influence of worldly goods is subtle and a snare to us. Everything of this world will pass away the Word of God tells us. We don't need more designer jeans; we need more contentment. Materialism and pleasure seeking are more of a problem in some areas of the world than others. I see many people caught in the trap of always wanting. The more they get the more they want.

Paul was well educated, rich, and a leader in the religious world. He had it all, but he tells us that he counted it nothing compared to Christ in his life. He learned how to be content with whatever he had and wherever he was (Philippians 4:11). God doesn't care if we own things, but He does care if things own us. I always measure my "things" in the scope of eternity. Speak and take authority over the demonic influence of materialism and pleasure seeking. Allow the Holy Spirit to fill us with His **contentment.**

PERIZZITES. The name means rustic or squatter. A squatter means someone who settles on something that does not belong to them. Doesn't IMMORALITY do that? Wanting what does not belong to us is running rampant in our society. Morality means principles of right or wrong. It is not only speaking of sexual right or wrong, but also of our integrity. Isaiah 5:20 says,

Woe to those who call evil good, and good evil; Who put darkness for light, and light for darkness; Who put bitter for sweet, and sweet for bitter! Isaiah is talking about moral subversion. The Bible teaches about right and wrong. Moral absolutes! Divorce is out of control. Marriage takes work and we can't just leave because we get tired of our partner! The enemy always wants us to think the grass is greener on the other side of the fence. Yes, God will forgive us for divorce and yes, there are Biblical reasons for divorce. But the higher law of God is He hates divorce, and He expects us to work at keeping our marriage together. Years ago there was a very popular song titled "I Did It My Way." Those are the exact words that messed up my life. I did do it MY WAY and messed up my life in a big way. I had what was right and what was wrong all messed up. We only have to look around us to see MORAL SUBVERSION everywhere. Speak to and take authority over the influence of immorality. Allow the Holy Spirit to bring integrity, which is **commitment** and **faithfulness,** to our lives.

HIVITES. This means villager or cave dweller. We cannot live the Christian life in a cave. A cave is dark and lonely. It has no light except that which comes from the outside. I have heard people say, "I am going to find a cave somewhere and stay in it." People who are deceived are people who have compromised at some point in their faith walk. The light of truth is missing in their life. Compromise is to water down what we know to be truth so it will please someone else or ourselves. Deception means to be tricked or misled. We cannot allow lethargy or tolerance to evil to remain in our life. People who live in a cave too long without light will become blind. It is the same with deception. ...*whose minds the god of this age has blinded, who do not believe* (2 Corinthians 4:4). The god of this age is Satan. He loves to blind or put a cover over our eyes to the things of God. A person who is deceived is just that–deceived. They don't know it or they would not be deceived. When we do not believe what the Word of God says, we will become blinded. James 1:22 goes further by saying, *But be doers of the word, and not hearers only, deceiving yourselves.* It is very dangerous to hear the Word or read the Word all the time and not apply it to our life. We are bringing on deception to ourselves. It is only the truth of the gospel that will set us free from deception and compromise. Speak to and take authority over the spiritual influences of deception and compromise. Allow the Holy

Spirit to shine the light of **truth** in our lives and fill us up.

JEBUSITES. The name means trodden down. To be trodden down means depressed! This was a big one in my life. I believed the lie, which told me that alcohol would solve my problem of depression. Alcohol would cause me to have a false high that would only last until the affects of the stuff wore off. Then I was really in the dumps. I was also on all kinds of pills for this problem. I was hounded by this problem for years before I became a child of God. Now I believe what the Bible says! *Anxiety in the heart of man causes depression* (Proverbs 12:25). *Hope deferred makes the heart sick* (Proverbs 13:12). These two verses took me out of my depressed condition. I learned that worry is anxiousness and when I get anxious, depression can come.

Hope means anticipate with pleasure! When I first came into the things of God my husband and son were not believers. If I allowed the thoughts to come saying my situation was always going to be the same, I would lose my hope and become depressed. I had to take thoughts captive that did not line up with the Word of God and cast them down. If I hadn't done that those thoughts would have taken me captive. Thoughts will progress to an imagination, and if thoughts are dwelt on long enough, they will become a stronghold in our mind. If we don't cast down thoughts that don't line up with the Word of God, we will soon have a demonic stronghold. If we line up our thoughts with the Word of God and **retain** them, we will have a Godly stronghold. One will cause depression; the other is an antidote for depression. Speak to and take authority over the demonic influence of depression. Allow the Holy Spirit to fill our lives with **encouragement** and **hope.**

We have to drive these spiritual influences out of our life before they become a stronghold. We are influenced each day by the demonic realm. The children of Israel were told to show these enemies no mercy and completely destroy them. They did not do what they were told and King Solomon even made servants out of those not destroyed. They were told that any enemies left would become a snare to them and they did. The nation was split in half during the time of Solomon's reign as king. We can't show these enemies in our life mercy or make servants out of them.

We must be honest and allow the Holy Spirit to show us the spiritual nations, which are influencing us. Each spiritual nation is a stumbling block put in front of us by Satan to keep us from the walk of faith. We can't think them away because thinking is not speaking. Evil spirits do not know what you are thinking; they will only respond to speaking. In the name of Jesus WE must drive them out and totally conquer them in order to have a life that shines with supernatural God-faith. Show them no mercy!

Chapter 19
FAITH AND OBEDIENCE
GO TOGETHER
Couple willingness to do God's
will with being obedient to do it

Things don't just fall into our lap. We have to believe for them. Faith has a lot to do with whether or not we receive the blessings of God. However, we must also be obedient to the things of God. Isaiah 1:19 records, *If you are willing and obedient, you shall eat of the good of the land.* If we combine willingness and obedience, He will prosper us, but we have to be willing and obedient to do what He wants us to do. Not one *or* the other. I had read this Scripture many times, but one day it came alive to me. At that moment my faith grew. Why? How did my faith grow?

There are two different words used for the Word of God. One is Logos, which means an expression of thought or the message; the written Word. The other is Rhema, which means the communication of the message with the words coming alive to us; the spoken word. All of a sudden the written Word "If you are willing and obedient" came alive and spoke to my heart, "Judy, if YOU are willing and obedient." When the written Word of God speaks to our heart, it will become personal with a personal choice to obey or not to obey.

I saw the "if" in that verse and the two conditions that would allow me to eat from the GOOD of the land. I had to couple willingness to do God's will with being obedient to do it. But I am also shown by the unsaid in the verse that if I don't fulfill both conditions, I won't eat from the good of the land. With Isaiah making the distinction of "the good of the land," I realized there had to be a "bad of the land." I wanted no part of the BAD. The Word tells us we will always have trials and tribulations, but in spite of them, we can eat from the good of the land. What does it mean eat? If we don't eat we will die. Eating keeps us alive. So eating from the good of the land will keep us alive. We can eat bad food or we can eat good food. What is the good of the land?

Micah 6:8 tells us, *He has shown you, O man, what is good; and what does the Lord require of you but to do justly, To love mercy, And to walk humbly with your God?* Here it shows us that the GOOD of the land is to have justice, mercy, and humility as we go through this journey of life with our Lord. Our choice! If we eat well, both spiritually and physically, we will be nourished and have a healthy journey. If we eat poorly, both spiritually or physically, we will be malnourished and not have a healthy journey through this life. Our heavenly Father wants us to be willing to do His will so we can enjoy being nourished with His justice, mercy, and humility as we travel this life fulfilling His purposes. I grabbed hold of this. We have to live what we preach. If I preach faith, I must live faith. Our lifestyle must be faith. Don't believe things have to stay the way they are. They don't. We can move the situation and the circumstances into the words that we say, if our words are in line with the Word of God. We must live faith in all areas of our life, and meet the conditions of the Word, not just the reasoning of our minds.

Faith is the same in every sphere of life—salvation, baptism in the Holy Spirit, finances, healing, relationships, careers—everything that relates to us. We must be willing and obedient, which will cause us to be yielded to the plan of God. I was obedient. I have been very obedient to the Word of God, to the will of the Father.

But I haven't always been that *willing* to be obedient. The Lord says I must have both to eat from the good of the land.

I had to make some corrections in my life. One of the hardest mission projects for me in the beginning was the one in Glendo, Wyoming. When my husband first mentioned this project I certainly was not willing to go do it. This project took me out of my familiar setting. The Bible camp is thirty miles from any significant town. It is located about four miles off the highway on a dirt road. The surrounding country is beautiful, but full of crawling or walking critters. I am a city girl, but my husband is a country boy. He does great with all this isolation and critters. I knew this was the mission project God wanted us to be on, and this Scripture in Isaiah 1:19 changed my life. I have seen the hand of God at work on this project. I started to eat of the good of the land. Everything we need is here. He has made it all for us. Not the devil. It belongs to us, the children of God. As a child of God I have to understand this. It all belongs to my heavenly Father. I am to partake of it and enjoy it.

In Psalm 50:10-12 our God says, *"For every beast of the forest is Mine, and the cattle on a thousand hills. I know all the birds of the mountains, and the wild beasts of the field are Mine. If I were hungry, I would not tell you; For the world is Mine, and all its fullness."*

The silver and the gold, the cattle on a thousand hills are all owned by our God and He made it all for us. The word meek does not mean weak, and being poor and downcast is not humility. *My people are destroyed for lack of knowledge...(*Hosea 4:6). This is talking to the believer! To have knowledge is to have an understanding of what the Word says. We must have a working knowledge of the Word of God. If we don't, it will destroy us! We do not have to be poor and we do not have to be depressed. Sometimes we are poor because if we had money we would walk in pride. I hear many say that Jesus was poor. Was He? If Jesus was poor, why did He have enough in the moneybox for one of His disciples to steal from Him? (John 12:6). Jesus was not concerned about having things. He was only concerned about doing the will of the Father. He is certainly the very best example of being "Willing and Obedient" we could have. When He needed things, they were provided.

Prosperity is not only money, but also peace, health, and joy, to name a few. We can have all the money in the world and not be happy or healthy. We need to avoid a poverty mentality and a riches mentality, and focus on having a Jesus mentality. A Jesus mentality says what the Word says.

The Lord will command the blessing on you in your storehouses and in all to which you set your hand, and He will bless you in the land which the Lord your God is giving you (Deuteronomy 28:8).

The Lord will open to you His good treasure, the heavens, to give the rain to your land in its season, and to bless ALL the work of your hand. You shall lend to many nations, but you shall not borrow (Deuteronomy 28:12).

And we know that all things work together for good to those who love God, to those who are the called according to His purpose (Romans 8:28).

…If God is for us, who can be against us? (Romans 8:31).

The list goes on and on. A Jesus mentality is a **faith** mentality. Our heavenly Father has given to us as His children everything we will need for this journey of faith through this life. He owns it all. But Paul tells us in 2 Corinthians 4:3,4 *But even if our gospel is veiled, it is veiled to those who are perishing, whose minds the god of this age has BLINDED….* A veil covers something and keeps it hidden, and unless the gospel or the good news about the redeeming power of Jesus

Christ penetrates our life, we are perishing. Jesus redeemed us from the power of the enemy. He paid the price on Calvary and gave us back all that was taken from humanity at the fall of man. What the first Adam lost, the last Adam (Jesus) gave back to us. The power is in the name of JESUS! He has given us the authority as His children to use that name to retrieve what the enemy has stolen.

Satan is blinding many people, even the children of God. Satan has and will continue to rob God's children of the blessing, but Jesus came to break his power over all things. God has provided everything we need to finish what He has told us to do. We have to step into the authority given to us and loose what we need out of Satan's hand.

Is God sovereign? Yes! But Jesus said He gave us the keys to the kingdom of Heaven (Matthew 16:19). Jesus won the victory for us, but we must enforce it.

First we have to come in line with the Word of God. If I am not an offering giver nor a tither, I can't claim prosperity. If I'm walking in unforgiveness, I can't claim prosperity and healing, so now we have to take the whole counsel of God and we have to be balanced with it. We have to meet the conditions of the Bible. We must be willing and obedient—then we eat of the good of the Land!

Chapter 20
BE WISE IN WHAT IS GOOD!
When we settle for better,
we will miss the best

1 Thessalonians 5:21 says, *Test all things; hold fast to what is good.* Test all things means to hold things in the light of the Word. *...be wise in what is good...* (Romans 16:19). All that looks good is not necessarily good, nor is all that looks bad necessarily bad. We need the wisdom of God to show us the difference. James 1:5 says, *If any of you lacks wisdom, let him ask of God, who gives to all liberally....* I ask for wisdom all the time. The enemy does not dangle things like drinking or drugs in front of me because I can't be enticed with those anymore. But he does dangle other things in front of my eyes–things that could look good to me. Some things are good, but we are not ready for them or we have not developed our faith level for them. We have to know how to tell the difference. The fastest way to crash is to take off running with a good vision that has not come from God. We might get a vision that in the natural would not seem to be a good idea, but

when we put it in light of the Word and ask God for His wisdom concerning it, we will often find that this is God's vision.

Vic and I have had many things presented to us to consider, from houses and job opportunities, to different places to minister. They were all "good" things, but were they what God wanted for us at the time? This is what we need to determine. When we settle for the better, we will miss the best. Sometimes we question what we believe the Lord is leading us to do. Maybe it doesn't make sense to us, but sooner or later we find out why it was the best thing. We have traveled across many states to minister in some remote place, and we have been awed at what God does there. The devil wants to destroy our faith and pull us out of the will of God. That is his goal!

When my husband and I were going into the ministry, we wanted to sell our house in Reno so we put a price on it. Winter was coming and it still had not sold. God knows the timing of everything. People told me the price was too high for that neighborhood so we lowered the price. Some people came to look at it but they didn't qualify for a loan. We decided when snow hit the ground, we were just going to lock up the home.

About that time, a church was having special meetings. After one service, the evangelist looked at me and said, "I have a word for you." I said, "Oh, good!" God sent me a word that confirmed what was in my heart. He said, "Don't lower the price of your home. Put it back up." I thought, "Wow!" So I did just that. Only one other couple came and they wanted the house. They did not dicker with us and the house sold at the original price! I learned from that experience. We need to stand fast, even though all the circumstances look like it can't happen.

Mark 11:24 says, *Therefore I say to you, whatever things you ask when you pray, believe that you receive them, and you will have them.* What do we believe? One–we believe in prayer; that's good, but it's not what Jesus says for us to believe. Two–in the Bible; that's good, but that is not what Jesus says to believe. Three–in the Holy Spirit; wonderful, but that too won't work here. Prayer changes things, but just believing won't work here. Jesus tells us that when we pray, believe that we *receive.* Here is a huge key! Receiving is a real stumbling block for people. We love to give, but it is hard to receive.

I used to have really bad allergies. I believed that I was healed and I *was* healed. Believe and

receive now, not after we see the symptoms
disappear. It took two weeks before I saw that
my sinuses were clear before I received my
healing. But I stood on that and I knew God was
going to heal the allergies. You see, after the
symptoms had disappeared, I didn't need to
believe for it any more. So, I had to believe that
I had received, while I was right in the middle of
the sneezing and blowing my nose.

When we pray, believe we will have whatever
we desire, if it's in line with the Word of God
and we're not going to use it or squander it on
selfish motives. Begin to say that from your
heart, because we believe it. If you don't believe
it, start saying it anyway, and you can school
yourself into faith. I believe that I receive what?
What will happen? The rest of the verse says,
"and you shall have." The having is going to
come, but the having doesn't come first. Belief
comes first, then the having. If you need having
first and believing second, this is not faith.

Romans 1:17 says, *The just shall live by faith.*
Everything we do must be by faith. To move
mountains, we need to believe according to
God's Word. We must speak according to God's
Word. Hold fast to what is good! Be wise in
what is good for us! When we pray believe that

we receive what we ask for. We possess mountain-moving supernatural God-faith. We can use our faith for the things we need.

Chapter 21
PUT FEET TO YOUR FAITH!
Don't quit! Keep pressing toward Jesus

Our Lord wants people to *pray everywhere, lifting up holy hands, without wrath and doubting* (1 Timothy 2:8). No doubting, no wrath—one for each hand. As we lift our hands to the Lord, it's an act of surrender. We surrender all we are and offer our bodies as a living sacrifice as we glorify the Lord with the fruit of our lips. If we do not have any fruit in our life, could it be that we have no fruit coming out of our mouth?

Three verses in the book of Luke show us how to worship.

A woman in the city who was a sinner, when she knew that Jesus sat at the table in the Pharisee's house, brought an alabaster flask of fragrant oil, and stood at His feet behind Him weeping; and she began to wash His feet with her tears, and wiped them with the hair of her head; and she kissed His feet and anointed them with the fragrant oil. Now when the Pharisee who had invited Him saw this, he spoke to himself, saying, "This Man, if He were a prophet, would know who and what manner of woman this is who is touching Him, for she is a sinner" (Luke

7:37-39).

The fragrant oil that this woman brought was extremely costly. And she came and poured out every drop of it until there was none left. It was totally emptied out. She brought all that she had and laid it at the Master's feet. She wiped His feet with the hair of her head and anointed Him. Anoint means consecrate, set apart. We are to sit at the feet of Jesus and pour ourselves out so that He can fill us up. This will release our faith. This is living faith. Our faith will increase and release as we worship our Lord and bow down in submission to who He is. Praise Him, give Him thanks for what He has done and for who He is.

The Hebrew people used to go back and remember and recite all the great things that God had done for them. They would remember all the way back when the Lord brought them out of Egypt. We need to go back and recite all the things that God has done for us in bringing us out of Egypt, from the miry muck, the clay that we were stuck in before we were saved. He brushed us off and cleaned us up and breathed life into us. As we rise up within that and remember those things He's done for us, this will release our praise and our faith. We will bow down in worship and we will go forth as doers of the Word, serving Him with a very grateful heart.

Mark 5:25-34 tells about a desperate woman with persistent faith.

Now a certain woman had a flow of blood for twelve years, and had suffered many things from many physicians. She had spent all that she had and was no better, but rather grew worse. When she heard about Jesus, she came behind Him in the crowd and touched His garment. For she said, "If only I may touch His clothes, I shall be made well." Immediately the fountain of her blood was dried up, and she felt in her body that she was healed of the affliction. And Jesus, immediately knowing in Himself that power had gone out of Him, turned around in the crowd and said, "Who touched My clothes?" But His disciples said to Him, "You see the multitude thronging You, and You say, 'Who touched me?'" And He looked around to see who had done this thing. But the woman, fearing and trembling, knowing what had happened to her, came and fell down before Him and told Him the whole truth. And He said to her, "Daughter, your faith (not His faith) has made you well. Go in peace, and be healed of your affliction."

There is a place of persistence in our faith. This passage relates to an account of a desperate woman whose healing was a result of great and persistent faith. Her faith! Her illness made her ceremonially unclean and disqualified her from mixing with crowds of people. She would have been stoned, so she was on a suicide mission. But she had nothing more to lose. She had spent all her money on many physicians, but nothing had helped. Some of us are at that place right now. Don't quit! Keep pressing toward Jesus. She chose to risk her life to touch Jesus. She was certain that if only she could touch His clothes, she would be made well. She is a wonderful example of supernatural God-faith. She had all the odds against her. Jesus did not rebuke her, but delayed His mission to the home of Jairus, whose daughter was dying, in order to assure her of healing and salvation. Then we know that Jesus later raised Jairus' daughter from the dead, but here He took time to minister to one with persistent faith. Such persistence is rewarded. It's not just a healing or any other work of God; it's earned by human effort. It rather illustrates the need to be bold in what we believe so not to be deterred by circumstances or discouragement from others. All things are possible to him or her who believes and receives!

In Mark 5:34 Jesus said, *"Your faith has made you well."* She wasn't praying. There were no hands laid on her. But she released her faith. Jesus was the point of contact, and He still is our point of contact. If we touch His garment, if we touch Him, He still fills the temple. He's within us. We are the temples of the Holy Spirit. We need to know that our point of contact is Jesus Christ and when we touch Him, our Savior, our Healer, our Deliverer, when we get our focus on Him, and we have the same persistence as this woman, we just know that we shall be made whole.

Another good example of the faith that is within us, through the strength of Jesus Christ, is the blind beggar, Bartimaeus, found in Mark's Gospel. Bartimaeus was outside of Jericho, sitting by the side of the road when Jesus and his disciples, along with many other people, passed by. Mark 10:46-52 records,

When he heard that it was Jesus of Nazareth, he began to cry out and say, "Jesus, Son of David, have mercy on me!" Then many warned him to be quiet; but he cried out all the more, "Son of David, have mercy on me!" So Jesus stood still and commanded him to be called. Then they called the blind man, saying to him, "Be of good cheer. Rise, He is calling you." And throwing aside his garment, he rose and came to Jesus. And Jesus answered and said to him, "What do you want Me to do for you?" The blind man said to Him, "Rabboni, that I may receive my sight." Then Jesus said to him, "Go your way, your faith has made you well." And immediately he received his sight and followed Jesus on the road.

Once again we see that he heard about Jesus. And when he heard, hope jumped within him because he had heard the things that Jesus was doing. He acknowledged Him as the Messiah, Son of David. He knew that He was the Messiah; He had the goods. The beggar acknowledged that Jesus had what he needed. He was a professional beggar. His livelihood came from begging. Now a great multitude was passing by, which meant the possibility for money and he decided to go for the healing. But all the people who were with Jesus warned him to be quiet. I'm sure he was dirty, he was making a lot of noise, because it said he cried out very loudly, "Jesus, Son of David, have mercy on me!" They said, "Shush, be quiet!" But that didn't stop him; he cried louder. "Son of David, have mercy on me!" That got Jesus' attention and Jesus stood still.

When we have persistence, Jesus will stand still. Then they called the blind man. The same people who told him to be quiet, told him now to come. Be of good cheer, rise, He is calling you, get up! He had to get up and go from the place where he was. He had sat there year after year after year, begging. He had been comfortable with the familiar, but he decided; it was his choice. He could have chosen not to get up and go for the money instead, but he didn't do that. He threw aside his garment that kept him warm during the winter. That garment meant something. It was his calling card for livelihood, but he rose and he threw it aside and went to Jesus.

Many of us need to throw things off–doubt, unbelief, bad words, bad attitudes, poverty, and sickness. They come around us like a cloak, like a garment and we need to throw them off and come to Jesus.

The blind man threw it. He didn't give it to a friend in case it didn't work. He didn't fold it up for a rainy day. He threw it away, even while he was still blind. He prophetically knew that Jesus was going to heal him. Jesus asked him, "What do you want?"

Jesus knew Bartimaeus was blind, everybody in the multitude knew he was blind. Doesn't it seem ridiculous for the Master to say, "What is it that you want me to do for you?" Jesus needs to know specifically what we want. What do you want? Be specific about what you want from Jesus. Jesus wanted him to get his thought pattern together. And the blind man said, "Rabboni, that I may receive my sight." You see the word "receive" there is very instrumental, very important. He had to receive it. We have to receive the things of God. Pray, believe, and receive our sight. Bartimaeus knew that he was going to receive it. And Jesus said, *"Go your way, your faith has made you well."* And immediately he RECEIVED his sight.

Bartimaeus grabbed hold of his healing, he received it and he didn't just go his own away. No, he followed Jesus on the road. He became a follower of Jesus. He was persistent, taking a risk, going against the crowd, being unique; he was very radical. His faith arose within him and he said, "I'm going to get what God has for me; the Messiah is passing by." You know his spirit leaped with hope, anticipation, and expectancy.

I had been a licensed manicurist for seven years when we stepped out in faith to go to Bible school. At graduation we knew that we had to GO preach the gospel. God had put America on our hearts with a missionary call. During our time at school I still had my manicuring license. When it was time to go on the road with the gospel I had a choice to make. Do I renew my manicuring license just in case this ministry stuff does not pan out or do I not? We were stepping out to live the life of faith knowing that nothing pleases God but faith. We also had a full understanding that anything that is not of faith is sin! Wow! I never renewed my license. Like the blind man, I threw away my garment of security, which would have always pulled me backwards, and clothed myself only with the garment of Praise!

It doesn't matter what you need from God. The faith principles are the same. Remember that hope is expectancy, anticipating with pleasure that it's going to happen. Jesus saw their faith, THEIR FAITH. They put feet to their SUPERNATURAL God-faith.

Chapter 22
DREAM BIG
Is what you're living for
worth Jesus' dying for?

I believe most of the things that God wants to teach us, He wants us to learn for ourselves. I heard that Mark Twain once said, *"A man that carries a cat by the tail, learns something he can learn no other way."* We have to decide for ourselves, we have to learn for ourselves, we have to answer for ourselves. We have to know that our faith will rise up. Are we going to be knocked down? Sure we are. Are we going to fail? Sure we are, but how we respond to failure and mistakes is one of the most important decisions we make every day. Failure doesn't mean that nothing has been accomplished. There is always the opportunity to learn something. What is in you will always be bigger than what is around you.

Everybody gets knocked down. It's how fast you get up that counts. Think again about the difference between Peter and Judas. They both betrayed Jesus. They had both spent around three years learning from His teachings. One repented and didn't allow his mistake to stop him from becoming one of the greatest preachers in the history of the church. His first sermon brought in 3000 to the kingdom of God. The other one felt remorse for what he had done but allowed his past mistake to kill him.

There is a positive correlation between spiritual maturity and how quickly a person rises above and learns from his failures and mistakes. The greater the degree of spiritual maturity, the greater the ability to get back up and go on. The lesser the spiritual maturity, the longer the individual will continue to hang on to the past failures. Every person knows someone who to this day is still held back by the mistakes made years ago. God never sees any of us as failures. He only sees us as learners who are successful because of the blood of Jesus Christ. Every child of God is called a believer but only those who go on to become learners of the Master are called disciples!

The key to letting go of past failures and mistakes is to learn the lesson and forget the details. Gain from the experience. But do not roll over and over again in your mind the minute-by-minute details of it. Build on the experience and go on with your life.

Those who won't take chances don't make advances. All great discoveries have been made by people whose faith ran ahead of their minds. Significant achievements have not been obtained by taking small risks on unimportant issues. Don't ever waste time planning, analyzing, and risking on small ideas. It is always wise to spend more time on decisions that are irreversible and less time on those that are reversible. We need to learn to stretch. To reach out where God is. We need to aim high and take risks. Abraham and Sarah received the promise of God, but they had to walk away from everything familiar to them straight into a life of RISK, which developed a lifestyle of supernatural God-faith in them before they saw the fulfillment of the promise. The world's approach is to look to the next year based on the last year. As Christians we need to reach to our potential, not reckon to the past. Those who make great strides are those who take chances and plan toward the challenges of life. Let's not be caught up in small matters, so that we can't take advantage of important opportunities. Stretch our faith out there. Most people spend their entire lives letting down buckets into empty wells. They continue to waste away their days trying to draw them up again.

This should never be for a child of God. *Therefore with JOY you will draw water from the WELLS of salvation* (Isaiah 12:3). Our wells are not empty; they are full of salvation with the water of the Word of God directing us, and I will use my joy to dip it out!

Choose today to dream big, to strive to reach the full potential of your calling. Choose to major on the important issues of life and not the unimportant. Is it in the scope of eternity? If it is, I'm going to stretch my faith and I'm going to grab hold of it. If it's not, I don't want to waste my time on it. I heard when Charles Finney would preach he would ask the question, "Is what you're living for worth Jesus' dying for?" Security and opportunity are total strangers. If an undertaking doesn't include faith, it's not worthy of being called God's direction. I don't believe that God would call any of us to anything that would not include dependency on Him—FAITH.

Jesus is the originator of our faith and He is the perfector of our faith! Dream big because we serve a big God.

Faith, Does It Really Move Mountains? Why don't you exercise your supernatural God-faith and see!

About the author

Several years ago, Judy and her husband, Vic, felt a strong call of God on their lives. They sold their successful businesses and home in Reno, Nevada, and moved to San Jose, California. There they lived in a 32-foot fifth wheel trailer for two years while they attended Bible College. While there God gave them a burden for America.

She and her husband are the Founders and Directors of Good News Ministries, Inc., which serves the mission field of America. In their reconstructed Greyhound bus, they travel the country introducing Jesus to those who don't know Him, reintroducing Jesus to those who once knew Him, and sharing more of Jesus with those who do know Him. They also reach out to help those in need with clothing and food.

Judy's sensitivity and obedience to the Holy Spirit brings restoration, healing and deliverance. As she flows in the Gifts of the Spirit, she ministers with simplicity, clarity, and accuracy to bring about change in peoples' lives!

She is the author of two books, *From Rags to*

Riches, and *Faith, Does it Really Move Mountains?*
She has also written numerous articles for
Christian publications. Judy is an ordained
minister, a Chaplain for Campers for Christ, and
a teacher at Jubilee International Training Center
in San Jose, California. She has her Associate
Degree in Biblical Studies, a Diploma of
Theology, and is currently finishing her
Bachelor's/Master's Degree in Theology.

* * *

Judy can be contacted through Good News
Ministries, Inc.:

Judy Baus
Good News Ministries, Inc.
9309 99W Hwy
Gerber, CA 96035
(530) 385-1271